W9-BGA-758

PALEO GREEN SMOOTHIES

150 Green Smoothie Recipes
FOR MAXIMUM HEALTH

MICHELLE FAGONE
of CavegirlCuisine.com

Adamsmedia

Avon, Massachusetts

Copyright © 2016 by F+W Media, Inc.
All rights reserved.
This book, or parts thereof, may not be reproduced in any form without permission from
the publisher; exceptions are made for brief excerpts used in published reviews.

Published by
Adams Media, a division of F+W Media, Inc.
57 Littlefield Street, Avon, MA 02322 U.S.A.
www.adamsmedia.com

Contains material adapted from *The Everything® Healthy Green Drinks Book*, by Britt Brandon, copyright
© 2014 by F+W Media, Inc., ISBN 10: 1-4405-7694-7, ISBN 13: 978-1-4405-7694-2.

ISBN 10: 1-4405-9293-4
ISBN 13: 978-1-4405-9293-5
eISBN 10: 1-4405-9294-2
eISBN 13: 978-1-4405-9294-2

Printed in the United States of America.

10 9 8 7 6 5 4 3 2 1

Library of Congress Cataloging-in-Publication Data
Fagone, Michelle, author.
Paleo green smoothies / Michelle Fagone of CavegirlCuisine.com.
pages cm
Includes index.
ISBN 978-1-4405-9293-5 (pb) -- ISBN 1-4405-9293-4 (pb) -- ISBN 978-1-4405-9294-2 (ebook) -- ISBN
1-4405-9294-2 (ebook)
1. Smoothies (Beverages) 2. Prehistoric peoples--Food. I. Title.
TX817.S636F34 2015
306.4--dc23
2015030434

Always follow safety and commonsense cooking protocol while using kitchen utensils and handling uncooked food. When using a blender, make sure the lid of the device is secured before turning it on. If children are assisting in the preparation of any recipe, they should always be supervised by an adult.

Many of the designations used by manufacturers and sellers to distinguish their products are claimed as trademarks. Where those designations appear in this book and F+W Media, Inc. was aware of a trademark claim, the designations have been printed with initial capital letters.

Cover photography and design by Alexandra Artiano.

This book is available at quantity discounts for bulk purchases.
For information, please call 1-800-289-0963.

Dedication

To my amazingly nutty and chaotic family . . . Sam, Samantha, Calla, Mom, and Dad. I love you. Thank you for always supporting my crazy endeavors!

CONTENTS

INTRODUCTION

If you are seeking out Paleo green smoothies, you may already be living the Paleo lifestyle. On the other hand, you may have heard about the Paleo diet but are not quite sure what it is. If you fall into this group, here's the basic idea: Those who follow this diet eat very clean and simple foods, eliminating grains, refined sugar, dairy, and legumes.

It is the oldest diet in the world. The Paleo lifestyle takes us back to our ancestors in the Paleolithic era, when humans hunted and gathered their food. Fish were caught, not farmed. Berries, nuts, and plants were foraged in their natural state. The simplicity and honesty of this food produced bodies free of inflammation.

Ridding your body of toxins found in many of the foods in the Standard American Diet (SAD) will lead to increased energy and stamina, better sleep, clearer skin, and sharper focus. The pain from arthritis and swollen joints in your body due to these inflammatory foods can be reduced or even eliminated. Your muscle growth and fitness levels will increase. Blood sugar levels will stabilize, resulting in reduced mood swings. These are just a few of the benefits you'll experience. Only good effects can come to those who choose to eat real foods free of additives, substances that have no place in the human body.

So how did the caveman get his hands on a blender and make green smoothies? Well, unless you intend to live in a cave with no technological advances, you'll have to adapt to modern-day Paleo. These days, to find produce and meats you only need to make a trip to the grocery store, butcher, or farmers' market. Choose local, in-season, organic produce as much as possible. You can grow veggies, fruits, and herbs in your home garden or even in pots on your deck. A lot of people don't have the time or inclination to hunt, so choose local farms that raise grass-fed, free-range animals. When you purchase a whole or half animal you can usually get a great price. The farmer will even break it down and neatly package the parts for you. Another tip is to become friends with the butcher. You're more likely to get the freshest cuts, special orders, and a little extra thrown in just for you.

Today's world is dominated by fast-food convenience. Everywhere you turn, there are reasons to eat chemically enhanced, preservative-ridden meals. We as a society no longer consume real foods but food-like substances. Granted, they are in pretty packages and use a lot of healthy buzzwords, but look at the ingredient lists. Go on! I double-dog dare you. Have you looked at one of those lists lately? It's scary. It's deplorable. It's SAD (pun intended).

Enter green smoothies. They are portable, easy to make, and can be hearty and filling. Smoothies are the new fast food. They are a quick way to get a shot of nutrients, minerals, and enzymes into your system. How often do we fill our plates with greens, carrots, blueberries, and the like? The answer for most is sometimes—or you may only consume one or two of these with your meal. Green smoothies allow you to blend multiple nutritional power foods together before heading out on the road for your myriad of errands. They are a wholesome alternative to fast food and honestly, they are just delicious. Embrace your inner hippie and just taste the health. Those happy place endorphins will be running through your body ready to help you conquer your world.

In Part 2 of this book, you'll find 150 easy-to-follow, simple-to-prepare Paleo green smoothie recipes, along with nutritional information on the produce used. Isn't it time to take responsibility for your health and live the best life possible? Yes it is . . . and yes, you're worth it!

PART 1
Paleo Green Smoothies 101

CHAPTER 1

What Is Paleo?

The Paleolithic diet or "Paleo" has become increasingly popular. Also known as the "Caveman Diet," it takes its name from a time when people only ate grass-fed game, wild-caught fish, nuts, vegetables, berries, and fruits. These people lived before modern agriculture and the domestication of animals. They hunted for meat and gathered berries and nuts. There were no grains planted in fields and there was no processed milk; as a result, the population wasn't plagued by many of the chronic diseases we see today such as obesity, diabetes, and osteoporosis. Granted, the cavepeople didn't have access to all of the produce in the recipes of Part 2, but they also didn't have access to blenders and grocery stores. Following a Paleo lifestyle is more about eating as close to the ground, if you will, as possible. It is about avoiding processed foods, eating pastured meats, and consuming organic produce as often as possible.

Even though they had to find or kill most of their food, your Paleolithic ancestors were still eating better quality foods than most of the world's population today. Not only are the hundreds of quick-fix weight-loss products wreaking havoc on the human body, but the Standard American Diet (SAD) with grains at its helm is believed to contribute to a number of diseases and weaknesses of our bodies.

Adherence to the Paleo lifestyle can also help in the prevention and management of chronic diseases. It also encourages a naturopathic-based and organic approach to health, as well as a greater ownership of your well-being. Being self-aware and establishing a more health-conscious perception of yourself is important in becoming and staying well.

Right now you're probably thinking that to live the Paleo lifestyle you need to move to the forest and take up hunting, fishing, and gardening. That couldn't be further from the truth. All that is required is a shift in thinking from the programmed "diet mentality" that has been impressed upon society for decades. Think fresh. Think whole foods. Think unprocessed.

Green smoothies are not only an enjoyable way to ease into the Paleo lifestyle; they are a great addition to your free-range, organic meals throughout the day. First-timers may be a little timid because some of the vegetables in these smoothies are a bit out of the ordinary. Don't worry. Green smoothies help blend flavors together for a delicious experience. Each of the greens,

herbs, fruits, and vegetables contains different nutrients and minerals. Each Paleo green smoothie packs a powerful medley of the vitamins and minerals that your body and mind need in order to work at their fullest potential.

Paleo green smoothies are easy to carry around while accomplishing your daily tasks. Smoothies keep your body loaded with clean fuel while helping your mind focus on whatever task is at hand.

We are a busy nation of worker bees. There isn't always an outdoor grill around the corner awaiting grass-fed meat and organic veggies. Preparation is a large percentage of living any healthy lifestyle; another advantage of smoothies is that prep takes little time. These recipes should help keep even the busiest person on track eating a wholesome diet rich in greens, fruits, and vegetables.

Whether you choose to drink green smoothies for post-workout meals, detoxification, anti-aging, or just everyday health, you'll find the right recipe in *Paleo Green Smoothies*. This book offers a broad variety of produce combinations and flavors. After making some of these tasty smoothies, in no time you'll be whipping up your own inspired creations. Good luck!

CHAPTER 2
Paleo Green Smoothie Basics

Whether you're looking for a meal replacement or a snack, the Paleo green smoothie offers a variety of produce that is typically not eaten at most meals. Think of it as a nutritional boost, an injection of health. When drinking a green smoothie as a meal replacement, choose recipes that have a dose of protein in the form of eggs, nuts, or nut butters.

Green smoothies are not meant to be a quick-fix remedy or for rapid weight loss. These goals run counter to the Paleo lifestyle. The main goal is to eat fresh, non-processed foods until you're satisfied. You won't need to count calories, step on a scale constantly, measure food, and obsess over your food choices. Just eat good, whole foods. They are filling and satisfying. There are no empty calories, foods providing calories but no nutritional benefit, like those found in robo-processed foods. Your body will thank you by producing shiny hair, a glowing face, reduced inflammation, increased energy, better sleep, and yes, weight loss. The amazing powers of healing and the countless benefits from consuming rich greens used in smoothies are astounding. Abundant vitamins, minerals, antioxidants, amino acids, omega-3s, healthy fats, phytochemicals, and proteins can change the natural processes of your body

for the better. All of these are unleashed in every Paleo green smoothie you consume.

Although the value of a diet rich in greens, fruits, and vegetables has been well known for quite some time, the green smoothie has not been commonplace until recently. It has also been only during the past couple of years that nutritionists have identified the Standard American Diet (SAD) as the main culprit in multiple health issues that strike people of all ages and backgrounds. With the breakthrough of Paleo, which focuses on whole, nutrient-dense foods, green smoothies can take their place as a perfect addition to this lifestyle.

What Are Paleo Green Smoothies?

A Paleo green smoothie is a mixture of greens, fruit, and sometimes additions such as seeds and nuts, blended together until a desirable, smooth texture is achieved. Although there are many smoothie combinations that target specific needs or areas of the body, the main reasons to consume green smoothies are:

- To eat more vegetables and fruits on a daily basis
- To enjoy the green smoothie combinations you choose from this book
- To create your own green smoothies blending your favorite flavors
- To live a healthier and happier lifestyle as a result of this major nutritional shift in your daily life

Integrating these smoothies into your average day without extra time, money, or hassle is easily done. It takes only minutes to prepare, blend, and enjoy these green treats, and it requires only a blender and the vegetables and fruits of your choosing. The entire process is easy to understand and apply to any schedule—no matter how hectic.

But not all smoothies are created equal. You can purchase smoothies in the grocery store, but the word "smoothie" in that case varies in meaning from what we've been talking about. Instead of the fresh, non-processed fruits and vegetables included in Paleo green smoothies, often labels for commercial smoothies state they contain 100 percent fruit juice, made with fruit juice, 100 percent natural fruit juice, and so on. Each description has a slightly different meaning in the eyes of the Food and Drug Administration (FDA). So, instead of trying to decipher the SAD codes, which are meant to trick us into buying "healthy" ingredients, put yourself in control by making your own green smoothies. That way you'll know exactly what is going into the delectable green drink. It is fresh and contains no concentrates, and the produce hasn't been pasteurized, a process that extends shelf life but ends up killing a large amount of the very nutrients you wanted to consume in the first place.

Greens and Nutrition

Paleo green smoothies are void of refined sugar and processed protein powders. Most people know that greens are very nutritious but struggle to eat enough of them—they're not the easiest vegetables to prepare tastefully while maintaining all of the important vitamins and minerals your body requires. Steamed, sautéed, baked, and roasted vegetables are certainly delicious; however, the heat causes them to lose some vitamins and minerals. As well, you may not gain the full benefits from your average meal or salad containing greens because the greens can be tedious to chew and difficult to digest. Blended greens in smoothies have already been ripped apart and are effectively "pre-digested," allowing for almost immediate absorption by your body.

Although many people suffer from digestive irregularity, few know the power of fiber contained in a serving of greens. A type of carbohydrate that resists the body's digestive enzymes and acids, soluble fiber forms a gel-like substance in the digestive tract that binds with cholesterol so it can't be reabsorbed by the body. Insoluble fiber (often referred to as "nature's broom") moves food through the digestive system more quickly, reducing instances of constipation. Increasing your daily intake of deep-green vegetables and certain fruits can make irregularity a thing of the past.

Symptoms and illnesses that arise from a vitamin deficiency make deep-green vegetables a one-stop shop for ensuring you fulfill your body's needs for vitamins. Paleo green smoothies negate any possible illnesses and symptoms that could arise from being vitamin deficient. Your body doesn't naturally produce the eight essential amino acids that we need for bodily functions such as muscle repair, manufacturing hormones, mental functions, sleep, memory, and physical and mental energy; you need to get them from the foods you consume.

Greens and Healing

Smoothies are healthful, but green smoothies . . . well, they are insanely healthful! Greens, especially dark leafy ones, purify the blood, provide energy through folate (a type of B complex vitamin), fight infection, build the immune system, boost brain function with vitamin K, and reduce the damage of free radicals, molecules created by stress and

pollution that lead to aging. And these benefits just scratch the surface. What a shame that a miracle pill that could accomplish all of this hasn't been offered at hundreds of dollars. Well, there is no need. Go directly to your blender. You win.

Each recipe in this book contains a handful or two of greens. You can substitute a favorite leaf for all the greens in these recipes. But do yourself a favor: If you've never tried some of the greens listed here, be adventurous. It is easy to get in a habit of only including your favorite greens, but try a mix. Not only does the nutritional benefit of each green vary, but the taste and texture differ also, offering limitless combinations when blended with other ingredients. Buying a bag of mixed greens is helpful to use on those extremely busy or even lazy weeks. No "thinking" needed. Throw a couple handfuls in with your favorite fruit/veggie/liquid combination and life is good.

Following are lists of some of the vitamins and minerals you can get from the greens in this book.

Vitamins

- Biotin. Found in deep-green leafy vegetables, biotin is responsible for cell growth, maintaining a steady blood sugar level, and the metabolism of fats and amino acids. It also strengthens hair and nails.
- Carotene. Vibrant orange and yellow vegetables and leafy greens get their color from this amazing vitamin that is a powerful antioxidant. It provides protection

from free radicals and aids in cancer prevention. Important phytochemicals lutein, lycopene, and beta-carotene are released with the tearing of these vegetables and provide the body with protection from illness and disease.

- Vitamin A. Carrots and dark-green and yellow vegetables hold this important vitamin, known for its role in aiding vision health and proper cell growth.
- Vitamin B1. Also known as thiamin, B1 aids in every process, including nervous system processes, muscle function, metabolism of carbohydrates, the production of healthy digestive enzymes, and electrolyte flow. This vitamin can be found in oranges and certain citrus fruits.
- Vitamin B2. Also known as riboflavin, this vitamin is found mainly in broccoli and asparagus. It aids cells in their growth, maintains proper cell functioning, and produces energy.
- Vitamin B3. Also known as niacin, this hormone-regulating vitamin assists the adrenal glands in production of sex- and stress-related hormones, lowers LDL ("bad" cholesterol) while raising HDL ("good" cholesterol), and has been recently suggested to alleviate symptoms of arthritis.
- Vitamin B5. Also known as pantothenic acid, this vitamin is responsible for synthesizing and metabolizing fats, carbohydrates, and proteins for all necessary bodily functions.
- Vitamin B6. Also known as pyridoxine, B6 is found in peas, carrots, and spinach and is responsible for the synthesis of important neurotransmitters serotonin and norepinephrine.
- Vitamin B12. Also known as cobalamin, this vitamin aids in blood formation and energy production and is necessary for the metabolism of every cell throughout the body.
- Vitamin C. Found in most citrus fruits and in vibrant-colored and deep-green vegetables, vitamin C is well known for its immune-boosting properties, but is also necessary for iron absorption and supports the growth and repair of cartilage, collagen, muscle, and blood vessels.
- Vitamin D. Produced in our bodies as a result of exposure to the sun, vitamin D from plant sources is needed to protect your body from autoimmune diseases, cancers, osteoporosis, and hypertension.
- Vitamin E. This fat-soluble antioxidant has been known for stimulating skin repair and strengthening cells, but it is also necessary in removing free radicals from the body's systems. It is found in abundance in spinach, collards, and dandelion greens, as well as in turnips and beets.
- Vitamin K. This fat-soluble compound is extremely helpful in blood clotting, and is found in the deep-green leafy vegetables.

Minerals

- Boron. Found in spinach, cabbage, and carrots, as well as apples, pears, and grapes, this mineral maintains the health of bones and teeth by metabolizing calcium, magnesium, and phosphorous. It has also been cited for building muscle and promoting mental clarity and brain functioning.

- Calcium. Although well known for maintaining the strength of bones and teeth, calcium also plays a vital role in maintaining regularity of the heart and helping to metabolize iron efficiently. Found in kale, broccoli, and collard greens, calcium is especially important for women who are pregnant, nursing, or menstruating.

- Chromium. This weight-loss helper is powerful in effective fatty-acid metabolism and works together with insulin to maintain the proper use of sugar in the body. Although broccoli is the best source of natural chromium, it can also be found in mushrooms, asparagus, bananas, and nuts.

- Copper. Found in most green vegetables, copper is another mineral that aids in the absorption of iron; it also helps to maintain cardiovascular health and can promote fertility in both men and women.

- Iron. Although all people require adequate amounts of iron found in dark-green vegetables, vegans and pregnant or menstruating women require much more iron. The reason iron is especially important for people who require additional protein is

that it is mainly responsible for strengthening the immune system and is found in great amounts in the proteins of red blood cells.

- Magnesium. This mineral is helpful in maintaining proper functioning of the muscles and the nervous system. Health problems resulting from low levels of magnesium include hypertension, diabetes, osteoporosis, and certain digestive disorders. Dark leafy greens such as spinach and collards are high in magnesium, but it can also be found in avocados, pumpkin seeds, and even dark chocolate.

- Potassium. Working with sodium to maintain a proper balance of the body's water, potassium is mainly required for the metabolism of carbohydrates and the synthesis of proteins. Some great sources of potassium include bananas, mangos, oranges, pears, and cantaloupe.

- Selenium. Found in deep-green vegetables (notably asparagus) and mushrooms, selenium aids weight loss by stimulating the metabolism. It is effective in disease prevention because it acts as an antioxidant against free radicals that cause health problems such as arthritis, cancer, and heart disease.

- Sodium. This mineral is important in maintaining proper muscle control and optimal nerve functioning, as well as correcting the body's distribution of fluid and maintaining proper pH balance. Some natural sources of sodium are beets, carrots, chard, and celery.

Preparation and Pantry Essentials

Preparing green smoothies gets easier once you've made a few. You will start to identify favorite greens, combinations, and add-ins. It will become second nature to put certain vegetables with particular fruits. The prep time required for the ingredients starts as soon as you get your greens, fruits, and vegetables home. Although greens will remain usable for days or weeks, their antioxidants, vitamins, and minerals dissipate from the time of picking. Eating them as soon as possible ensures you are getting the most nutrition out of every ounce. Below are the essentials you will need to make green smoothies.

- Produce. Choose the most seasonal, local, organic, and ripe produce. It has more flavor. Produce coming from a different state or country is generally picked early to allow for ripening time during shipping. The longer something is allowed to grow, the more intense its natural flavors. You can also buy frozen organic fruits that have been frozen ripe, are already diced, and act as flavorful little ice cubes for your smoothies.
- Blender. The top three points to consider when buying a blender to make smoothies are capacity, power, and price. Capacity: Will it hold all of your recipe ingredients? Power: You may want to consider wattage and various speed options. A blender with minimal strength may have a hard time breaking down ice cubes and hearty fruits and vegetables. It may require a smaller dice on fruits and grating some harder vegetables such as carrots. Price: This can be the deciding factor for many. Is it worth it? Do you really need the Mac Daddy of blenders, a high-horsepower emulsifying machine, or is one in the middle-of-the-road price range just fine? You'll find plenty of consumer feedback online for each type of blender. Do your homework before purchasing and your decision will be a lot easier.
- Knife. The most dangerous tool in the kitchen is a dull knife. With all of the dicing and chopping you'll be doing, find a good knife that works for you. An 8" chef's knife is the most versatile but if you have the moolah, invest in a whole set . . . right down to a tomato knife.
- Cutting board. Don't forget to pick up a cutting board. Whether it is wood, plastic, or bamboo, save your countertop the scratches and make this a kitchen staple.
- Strainer. A large strainer or veggie colander is a helpful kitchen tool. Some models fit right across the kitchen sink to make draining less messy. As soon as you return from shopping, thoroughly wash all produce and start the smoothie prep. With the produce washed, peeled, pitted, diced, and whatever else needs to be done, your Paleo green smoothie should only take 2–3 minutes from start to cup.

- Storage containers. There are plenty of glass storage containers available on the market that are perfect for storing and/or freezing prepped produce. There are also plastic varieties; however, be mindful of bisphenol A (BPA). It is a substance that can leach into your food and has caused multiple health concerns. If you choose plastic, seek out BPA-free containers.
- Travel mugs. After blending your green smoothie, you can take it to go in any insulated container that will help maintain its temperature and freshness. Or you can store it in an airtight glass container in your refrigerator for up to three days (although you'll probably drink it all before then).

CHAPTER 3
Key Ingredients

Deep-green organic produce is the best choice for your green smoothies. Creating green smoothies with organic fruits and vegetables ensures your tasty treat is free of dyes, pesticides, and preservatives. If you're concerned about the "priceyness" of organic produce, consider growing fruits and vegetables in your backyard garden. It is probably the easiest way to save money while also ensuring your ingredients haven't been contaminated by the dangerous herbicides or pesticides used in commercial agriculture, and you'll get maximum nutrients from the fresh fruits and vegetables you use. If you don't have the time or space to grow your own, purchase locally or regionally grown organic produce in your local health-food store, farmers' market, or supermarket. You can also prioritize your organic purchases by concentrating on the Dirty Dozen, the twelve most frequently contaminated items. The Dirty Dozen consists of peaches, apples, sweet bell peppers, celery, nectarines, strawberries, cherries, pears, grapes, spinach, lettuce, and potatoes.

Leafy Greens

Your green smoothie isn't complete without a dose of vibrant leafy greens. Research shows that leafy greens are one of the most concentrated sources of nutrition. They supply iron, calcium, potassium, magnesium, vitamins K, C, E, B6, and B12, and folate in abundance.

Leafy greens provide a variety of phytonutrients, including beta-carotene and lutein, which protect cells from damage and eyes from age-related problems. A few cups of dark green leaves also contain small amounts of omega-3 fatty acids and nine times the RDA for vitamin K (which regulates blood clotting). Greens protect bones from osteoporosis and may diminish the risk of atherosclerosis by reducing calcium in arterial plaques.

Types of Greens

Leafy greens run the gamut in taste, from arugula—which ancient Romans considered an aphrodisiac because of its peppery taste—to iceberg lettuce, which is crunchy and sweet with a very mild flavor. Here are some of the most popular leafy greens used for smoothies:

- Butter, Boston, or Bibb lettuce. Packed with vitamins A, C, and K, these three varieties of lettuce are almost indistinguishable. Similar in flavor and appearance, there are some scientific reasons why these three have different names, but for smoothie purposes, you can easily substitute one for another in recipes. Wash, and refrigerate up to 4 days.
- Collard and mustard greens. Both greens are packed with vitamins A, C, E, and K, making them powerhouses loaded with cancer-fighting properties. To store, wash greens thoroughly to remove dirt. Store cleaned greens in a plastic bag with as much air removed as possible, and refrigerate for up to 4 days.
- Frisée and escarole. Both are from the endive family. Frisée is the curly leafed, light-green variety with a mild flavor, whereas escarole is a more broad-leafed deep green that can be bitter if not

selected carefully. Both varieties are high in vitamins A and K, folate, and beta-carotene and are known for fighting depression and calming food cravings. Wash, and refrigerate up to 4 days.
- Green lettuce. Green lettuce such as romaine, iceberg, and green leaf is a good source of calcium, chlorophyll, iron, magnesium, potassium, silicon, and vitamins A and E. All types help rebuild hemoglobin, add shine and thickness to hair, and promote hair growth. Iceberg contains natural opiates that relax the muscles and nerves. Wash thoroughly, refrigerate, and use within 4 days.
- Parsley. Packed with chlorophyll, vitamins A and C, calcium, magnesium, phosphorous, potassium, sodium, and sulfur, parsley helps stimulate oxygen metabolism, cell respiration, and regeneration. Wash, refrigerate, and use within 5 days.
- Sorrel. Also known as spinach dock and actually classified as an herb, sorrel has a uniquely bright and sour flavor. It contains fiber and traces of protein. It is rich in vitamins C, A, B6, iron, and magnesium. Sorrel helps aid in eyesight, boosting metabolism, lowering blood pressure, and improving kidney health. Wash thoroughly and bag loosely in the refrigerator. Use within 4 days.
- Spinach, kale, and Swiss chard. Popeye was right: You'll be strong to the finish if you eat your spinach, kale, and chard, which are similar in nutritional value and provide ample supplies of iron,

phosphorous, fiber, and vitamins A, B, C, E, and K. Wash thoroughly and bag loosely in the refrigerator. Use within 4 days.

- Watercress. This delicate, leafy, green veggie has a slightly pungent taste and is packed with vitamin C, calcium, and potassium. It also contains acid-forming minerals, which make it ideal for intestinal cleansing and normalizing, and chlorophyll, which stimulates metabolism and circulatory functions. Refrigerate and use within 5 days.

Cruciferous Veggies

From broccoli and cauliflower to Brussels sprouts, kale, cabbage, and bok choy, the members of the cruciferous or cabbage family pack a nutritional wallop. They contain phytochemicals, vitamins, minerals, and fiber that are important to your health. Studies show that sulforaphane—one of the phytochemicals found in cruciferous vegetables—stimulates enzymes in the body that detoxify carcinogens before they damage cells.

Here's a rundown of the most delicious and nutritious cruciferous crops:

- Broccoli. Packed with fiber to help regularity, broccoli is also surprisingly high in protein, and it's full of calcium, antioxidants, and vitamins B6, C, and E. Because of its strong flavor, broccoli works best combined with other vegetables in juices, rather than juiced alone.

Wash thoroughly and use within 4 days to get maximum nutrients.

- Cabbage. Another member of the fiber-filled cruciferous family, cabbage comes in many different varieties, including white, red, and green cabbage, and Savoy cabbage with its delicate, crinkly leaves. Other members of the cabbage family you can use in your smoothies include Brussels sprouts, Chinese cabbage, and bok choy. All have large stores of vitamins B6 and C. Kale and collard greens also have a lot of vitamin A and calcium. Members of the cabbage family are also packed with minerals. Wash thoroughly and use within 4 days to get maximum nutrients.
- Cauliflower. Like other cruciferous vegetables, cauliflower has a strong flavor so it works best as a contributing player rather than a solo act. High in vitamin C and fiber, it has a more delicate taste than other cruciferous veggies. Wash thoroughly and use within 4 days to get maximum nutrients.

Root Vegetables

Classified by their fleshy underground storage unit or root, which is a holding tank of nutrients, root vegetables are low in fat and high in natural sugars and fiber. Root veggies are also the perfect foods to eat when you need sustained energy and focus.

Some of the most nutritious root veggies include those with orangey skins, such as carrots, squash, and sweet potatoes. The orange skin signifies they contain beta-carotene, a powerful antioxidant that fights damaging free radicals.

Here are some delicious and nutritious root vegetables to include in your smoothies:

- Beets. Both the beet greens and beet-roots are blendable and highly nutritious. The roots are packed with calcium, potassium, and vitamins A and C. Choose small to medium beets with fresh green leaves and roots. Use greens within 2 days and beets within 2 weeks.
- Carrots. Carrots lend a mild, sweet flavor to smoothies and taste equally delicious on their own. Carrots are rich in vitamins A, B, C, D, E, and K, as well as calcium, phosphorous, potassium, sodium, and trace minerals. Carrots stimulate digestion, improve the quality of hair, skin, and nails, have a mild diuretic effect, and cleanse the liver, helping to release bile and excess fats. Remove foliage when you get home, because it drains moisture and nutrients from the carrots. Refrigerate and use within a week.
- Celery. High in vitamin C and potassium with natural sodium, celery has a mild flavor that blends well with other veggies. Its natural sodium balances the pH of the blood and helps the body use calcium better. Choose firm, bright-green stalks with fresh green leaves. Refrigerate for up to a week.

- Fennel. Similar to celery in nutrients and high in sodium, calcium, and magnesium, fennel has a licorice-like taste that enhances the taste of juices made from vegetables with a strong flavor. Choose fennel bulbs the size of tennis balls with no bruising or discoloration. Refrigerate and use within 5 days.
- Garlic. A member of the lily family, this aromatic bulb, high in antioxidants for reducing cholesterol and heart disease, adds flavor and tang. Use 1–2 cloves per quart. Choose firm, smooth heads and store in a cool, dry place. Use within 2 weeks.
- Ginger. Technically a rhizome and native to Asia, ginger has a spicy, peppery flavor that enhances juice. Ginger has been revered for relieving gastrointestinal distress as well as helping pregnant women ward off nausea, but due to compounds called gingerols, it also is an anti-inflammatory in arthritis patients. Buy large, firm nodules with shiny skin. Refrigerate and use within a week.
- Green onions. Green onions are high in disease-fighting antioxidants and have the mildest flavor of the onion family, making them ideal for blending. They also have antibacterial properties that fight infections and skin diseases. Green onions should be firm and deep green in color. Refrigerate, and use within a week.
- Parsnips. Cousins to the carrot, parsnips are packed with vitamin C, potassium, silicon, and phosphorous. Choose large,

firm parsnips. Because there seems to be some science pointing to the toxicity of the greens of parsnips, they are usually sold without them. If growing them yourself, make sure to discard the top greens. Refrigerate and use within a week.

- Radishes. Small but mighty in taste and loaded with vitamin C, iron, magnesium, and potassium, radish juice cleanses the sinuses and gastrointestinal tract and helps clear up skin disorders. Use a handful to add zing to your smoothies. Refrigerate and use within a week.
- Sweet potatoes and yams. High in beta-carotene, vitamin C, calcium, and potassium, these two vegetables have a similar taste and can be substituted for one another in recipes. Store at room temperature and use within a week.
- Turnips and turnip greens. Ounce for ounce, turnip greens have more calcium than milk. The root supplies your body with calcium, potassium, and magnesium. Together, turnips and their greens neutralize overly acidic blood and strengthen bones, hair, nails, and teeth. Store turnips at room temperature, scrub well, and use within 2 weeks. Refrigerate greens and use within a week.

Veggies from the Vine

From acorn squash to zucchini, vegetables straight from the vine deliver a cornucopia of nutrients and fiber. Vine vegetables are also especially easy to grow in small, compact gardens or in containers on patios.

Here are some delicious and nutritious vegetables from the vine to include in your smoothies:

- Bell peppers. High in vitamin C, red bell peppers are also high in vitamin A and are much sweeter than the green variety. Bell peppers contribute to beautiful skin and hair; red bell peppers stimulate circulation and tone and cleanse the arteries and heart muscle. Wash peppers thoroughly and store in the vegetable crisper of the refrigerator for up to a week.
- Cucumbers. With their mild flavor, cukes compliment other vegetables and go well with herbs. Cucumbers are high in vitamin A and silica, which help repair connective tissue and skin. Buy firm, dark-green cucumbers with a slightly bumpy skin. Use within 4 days.
- Summer squash and zucchini. Rich in vitamin B, niacin, calcium, and potassium, summer squash and zucchini have a bland flavor that works best in combination with other vegetables. They help cleanse and soothe the bladder and kidneys. Store in a cool, dry place. Use within a few weeks.
- Tomatoes. Tomatoes are a good source of lycopene, which has been proven to have anticancer properties, and vitamin C and potassium, which cleanse the liver and add to the body's store of minerals, especially calcium. Fresh tomato juice

also stimulates circulation. Store at room temperature and use within the week.

Berries

Red, blue, purple, or black—no matter what the color or size, berries are wonder foods that are loaded with phytochemicals, antioxidants, and other vitamins and minerals that help prevent cancer and many other diseases. Cranberries and blueberries also contain a substance that may prevent bladder infections.

- Blueberries and blackberries. Both berries are packed with saponins, which improve heart health, as well as disease-fighting antioxidants, vitamin C, minerals, and phytochemicals. Refrigerate dry, fresh blueberries and blackberries immediately and use within a few days as they are very perishable. Wash thoroughly before using.
- Cranberries. High in vitamins C, B complex, A, and folic acid, cranberries help prevent bladder infections by keeping bacteria from clinging to the wall of the bladder. Cranberries help reduce asthma symptoms, diarrhea, fever, fluid retention, and skin disorders, as well as disorders of the kidney, urinary tract, and lungs. Cranberries also facilitate weight loss. Wash fresh cranberries thoroughly and refrigerate covered for up to 4 weeks.
- Raspberries. Raspberries provide plenty of vitamin C, potassium, and contain only 64 calories per cup. Refrigerate dry, fresh raspberries immediately and use within a few days as they are very perishable. Wash thoroughly before using.
- Strawberries. Strawberries contain lots of vitamin C, iron, calcium, magnesium, folate, and potassium—essential for immune system function and for strong connective tissue. Refrigerate dry, fresh strawberries immediately and use within a few days as they are very perishable. Wash thoroughly before using.

Tree Fruits

Fruits of the tree provide an abundance of life-enhancing and disease-fighting vitamins, minerals, antioxidants, and phytochemicals. Tree fruits are highly versatile players in making green smoothies naturally sweet and palatable, contributing a wide range of flavors, colors, and textures.

Here are some of the most popular fruits to use in smoothies:

- Apples. Rich in vitamins A, B1, B2, B6, C, folic acid, biotin, and a host of minerals that promote healthy skin, hair, and nails, apples also contain pectin, a fiber that absorbs toxins, stimulates digestion, and helps reduce cholesterol. Apples blend well with other juices.
- Apricots. Apricots are high in beta-carotene and vitamin A, and are a good source of fiber and potassium.
- Cherries. Rich in vitamins A, B, C, folic acid, niacin, and minerals, cherries are

potent alkalizers that reduce the acidity of the blood, making them effective in easing gout, arthritis, and prostate disorders.

- Grapefruit. Rich in vitamin C, calcium, phosphorous, and potassium, the pink and red varieties of grapefruit are sweeter and less acidic than white grapefruit. Grapefruit helps strengthen capillary walls, heal bruising, and reduce skin colds, ear disorders, fever, indigestion, scurvy, varicose veins, obesity, and morning sickness.
- Grapes. High in caffeic acid, which helps fight cancer, grapes are also packed with bioflavonoids, which help the body absorb vitamin C. Grapes also contain resveratrol, a nutrient that helps prevent liver, lung, breast, and prostate cancer, and saponin, a nutrient that binds with cholesterol and prevents the body from absorbing it.
- Lemons. Lemons are high in citric acid and vitamin C, so a little goes a long way in juicing. Their high antioxidant content and antibacterial properties relieve colds, sore throats, and skin infections and also help reduce anemia, blood disorders, constipation, ear disorders, gout, indigestion, scurvy, skin infections, and obesity.
- Limes. Similar to lemons in nutrients but not as acidic or cleansing, limes can be substituted for lemons in smoothie recipes.
- Oranges. A rich source of vitamins C, B, K, biotin, folic acid, amino acids, and minerals, oranges cleanse the gastrointestinal tract, strengthen capillary walls, and benefit the heart and lungs. Oranges help reduce anemia, blood disorders, colds, fever, heart disease, high blood pressure, liver disorders, lung disorders, skin disorders, pneumonia, rheumatism, scurvy, and obesity.
- Peaches and nectarines. High in beta-carotene and vitamins B and C, niacin, and minerals, peaches and nectarines cleanse the intestines and help relieve morning sickness.
- Pears. Rich in fiber and vitamins C and B, folic acid, niacin, and the minerals phosphorous and calcium, pears help reduce disorders of the bladder, liver, and prostate as well as constipation.
- Plums. High in vitamins C and A, copper, and iron, the benzoic and quinic acids in plums are effective laxatives. Plums help with anemia, constipation, and weight loss.
- Pomegranates. High in vitamins C, K, and folate, pomegranates contain antioxidants and phytochemicals that can protect your heart, keep your teeth clean, and even help reduce the risk of breast cancer. Pomegranates also aid in treatments associated with varying ailments of aging due to inflammation such as Alzheimer's and heart disease.

Melons

Melons are the juiciest fruit by far, and that makes them naturals for fresh smoothies. They come in many varieties, including canary, cantaloupe, cassaba, Crenshaw, honeydew, and mush. They are sweet and fun summertime thirst quenchers.

All varieties are rich in vitamins A, B complex, and C and promote skin and nerve health. Melons provide enzymes and natural unconcentrated sugars that help aid digestion.

- Cantaloupe is high in beta-carotene, vitamin C, and potassium. It alleviates disorders of the bladder, kidney, and skin and reduces constipation. Cantaloupes can be stored up to 2 weeks at room temperature. The hotter the room, the quicker the ripening. Once ripe, cut melon and refrigerate up to 1 week.
- Honeydew is high in potassium and vitamin C. When blended into smoothies, it promotes energy. It alleviates disorders of the bladder, kidney, and skin and reduces constipation. Honeydews can be stored up to 2 weeks at room temperature. The hotter the room, the quicker the ripening. Once ripe, cut melon and refrigerate up to 1 week.
- Watermelon is high in electrolytes and rich in vitamin A and the mineral potassium. It quenches thirst and also helps cleanse the kidney and bladder. Watermelon helps reduce discomfort associated with aging, arthritis, bladder disorders, constipation, fluid retention, kidney disorders, pregnancy, prostate problems, and skin disorders and promotes weight loss. Watermelons can be stored up to 2 weeks at room temperature. The hotter the room, the quicker the ripening. Once ripe, cut melon and refrigerate up to 1 week.

Tropical Fruit

You can find a bounty of tropical fruit in your local supermarket, even if you live in a cold climate. Try these in smoothies:

- Avocados. Although frequently mistaken for a vegetable, the avocado is actually a member of the pear family. Avocados are rich in vitamins A, C, and E. Ripe avocados can be refrigerated for up to 5 days.
- Bananas. Bananas are a great source of potassium, an essential electrolyte, as well as magnesium and vitamin B6. Store bananas on the shelf for several days. If you purchase them green, place them in a brown paper bag to speed up the ripening process. To slow down the process, refrigerate.
- Kiwi. Kiwis are rich in vitamins A and C and contain nearly as much potassium as bananas. Their fuzzy skins contain valuable antioxidants and can also be used in marinades for tenderizing meats. Kiwis can be kept up to 3 days at room temperature or refrigerated.
- Mangos. Like other orange-colored produce, mangos are packed with beta-carotene. Keep mangos at room

temperature until ripened and then refrigerate for a few more days.

- Pineapple. A great source of potassium, calcium, iron, and iodine, fresh pineapple is worth the hassle required to prepare it for smoothies. Using a strong knife, slice off the top and bottom of the pineapple so it sits flat on your cutting board, and then slice off the peel. Store pineapples at room temperature if they are not ripe (hard). Once ripened, cut and refrigerate for up to 3 days.

Other Additions

You can boost the taste and nutritional value of your green smoothies with herbs and a variety of liquids.

Herbal Additions

Herbs lend phytochemicals, fresh taste, and aroma to smoothies.

- Basil provides vitamins C and A, plus beta-carotene.
- Chives contain calcium, phosphorous, vitamins A and C, folate, niacin, riboflavin, and thiamin.
- Cilantro is renowned for its anti-cholesterol, anti-diabetic, and anti-inflammatory effects.
- Dill is rich in antioxidants and dietary fibers that help control blood cholesterol levels.
- Mint, including peppermint and spearmint, has the ability to cut off the blood supply to cancer tumors.

- Oregano is among the best sources of vitamin K, and it has antioxidants that prevent cellular damage caused by oxidation of free radicals.
- Rosemary provides carnosic acid, which shields the brain from free radicals and lowers the risk of stroke and neurodegenerative diseases.
- Tarragon is packed with minerals and vitamins C, B6, A, and E, and may help transfer nutrients to your muscles.

Freeze Your Herbs

To prevent herbs from going bad, freeze them. Remove fresh leaves from stems and chop them up. Place them in an ice tray. Fill sections with water and freeze. Once frozen, remove cubes from trays and place them in a labeled bag or container. Now they are ready to be used in smoothies, soups, sauces, or any one-pot wonder.

Other Additions

Many additional ingredients can enhance the taste and nutritional profile of a Paleo green smoothie. The bottom line is that what you need in your pantry is what you would like in your green smoothie. Try one ingredient, or try them all—it's up to you. Here are some suggestions:

- Almond butter. Almond butter is full of protein, healthy fats, fiber, and vitamins. Although it can be purchased, almond butter is simple to make. In a small food processor, blend a couple of handfuls of almonds and a pinch of sea salt until a paste forms. If you stop short of the paste, then you have almond meal/flour, which is used in many Paleo recipes and even some of the smoothies in this book. Almond butter is a great addition to Paleo green smoothies not only because of the nutritional value but because it also adds some creaminess to the mix.

- Coconut milk. Coconut milk is simply coconut meat and coconut water. Period. Be mindful of labels when purchasing coconut milk as some brands add emulsifiers and fillers. Stay away from the "light" varieties as this takes away from the natural healthy fats found in coconut and is counter to the whole-food mentality. Remember, fat doesn't make you fat. Sugar makes you fat.

- Coconut oil. Coconut oil is a healthy fat that can be added to your smoothies to help boost your metabolism. Composed mostly of triglycerides, coconut oil is easily digested and sent straight to the liver for energy production.

- Coconut water. Coconut water is the liquid from young green coconuts. Reading labels is important—avoid those brands that add fillers. If you're a purist and true cavegirl, buy a whole coconut, break out your machete (or hammer and chisel), and get your own fresh coconut water.

- Goji berries. Containing vitamins C and E, these tart little pink berries are rich in antioxidants that aid in boosting metabolism and regulating high blood pressure.

- Nuts and seeds. Before adding them to your smoothie, soak nuts and seeds overnight to help wash away the naturally occurring anti-nutrients such as phytic acid and tannins. Soaking also increases the potency of vitamins and helps with the growth of healthy enzymes necessary for healthy digestion.

- Unsweetened almond milk. Rich in copper, manganese, magnesium, potassium, vitamin E, selenium, and calcium, almond milk offers a strong healthy protein-packed alternative to cow's milk. Using almond milk in a green smoothie will lend a nutty background taste. Because store-bought almond milk can be full of additives and emulsifiers, follow these simple directions to create your very own homemade almond milk:

Recipe for Almond Milk

Grind ½ cup of almonds and a pinch of sea salt in a small food processor until fine. Blend with a cup of water for up to 3 minutes. Strain out remaining almond bits using a sieve or coffee filter.

- Teas. Brewed, cooled teas, caffeinated or not, green or black, can add depth of flavor to your Paleo green smoothies. Teas are also known to have a variety of medicinal and pampering effects. Substitute cooled teas for water in any of your smoothies. You can also freeze some in ice cube trays. This will allow you to add them to your smoothies without watering down the drink.

PART 2
Paleo Green Smoothie Recipes

CHAPTER 4
Breakfast Smoothies

Rise 'n shine! You're on the Paleo diet, your body is feeling energetic, and you're probably sleeping better and longer than ever before. Even with this extra skip in your step, some mornings you may not feel like cooking or even going through the motions. Enter the blender and the good ol' breakfast green smoothie. These drinks are delicious, nutritious, and easy to make. Although best to consume immediately due to nutrient loss, green smoothies can be refrigerated in an air-tight container for up to 48 hours. In this chapter you will find several different flavor combinations to start the day . . . even a Green Eggs and Bacon Smoothie for die-hard Paleo folks. I couldn't not include bacon in a Paleo book . . . it would be a cardinal sin. But, if "normal" is your thang, then go straight for the delicious Sunrise Smoothie.

If you are using these smoothies for a meal replacement, make sure you are getting some protein, either in your drink or on the side, especially if you are active. Now, go drink up and tackle your day with reckless abandon!

A Berry Healthy Morning Smoothie

Wake up to this beautiful glassful of berries that are packed with nutrients, vitamins, fiber, and antioxidants. Every berry is filled with phytonutrients that help to stave off free radicals, but each one also offers something unique and different. Don't be shy about switching up the ingredients below with some goji berries, strawberries, cranberries, or whatever you may find in your overfilled Community Supported Agriculture (CSA) box this week.

Recipe Yields: 3–4 cups

2 cups mixed baby greens
1 cup frozen raspberries
1 cup frozen blueberries
1 banana, peeled
2 cups unsweetened almond milk

1. Combine all ingredients and blend on high until smooth.
2. Add more liquid if necessary.

NUTRITIONAL INFORMATION (PER SERVING SIZE):

CALORIES:	FAT:	PROTEIN:	SODIUM:	CARBOHYDRATES:	SUGAR:	FIBER:
79	1.5 grams	1.7 grams	97 milligrams	16.4 grams	8.4 grams	4.3 grams

Green Eggs and Bacon Smoothie

This smoothie is for the true caveman or cavegirl. There was no way that I could exclude bacon from this book with the word "Paleo" on the front cover. This smoothie is a perfect pre- or post-workout meal to start your day with plenty of protein and antioxidants. Pastured eggs are defined as eggs laid by chickens that are allowed to roam free eating their natural food choices supplemented with some commercial feed.

Recipe Yields: 3–4 cups

2 cups baby spinach
2 slices crispy bacon
2 large pastured eggs from free-range hens
1 peeled and frozen banana
1 cup frozen blueberries
1 tablespoon pure maple syrup
2 cups coconut milk, chilled

1. Combine all ingredients on high until smooth.
2. Add more liquid if necessary.

NUTRITIONAL INFORMATION (PER SERVING SIZE):

CALORIES:	FAT:	PROTEIN:	SODIUM:	CARBOHYDRATES:	SUGAR:	FIBER:
347	26.6 grams	7.7 grams	130 milligrams	19.1 grams	10.0 grams	2.1 grams

Citrus Jump-Start Smoothie

Is there anything tastier than fresh orange juice in the morning? You betcha! This smoothie is packed with extra flavor and nutrients. As a society, we spend billions of dollars on miracle lotions, when all the while the fountain of youth is right at your fingertips. Couple fresh, organic smoothies with daily moderate exercise and you should be celebrating your twenty-first birthday again soon.

Recipe Yields: 3–4 cups

1 cup mixed greens
1 cup sorrel
3 oranges, peeled and seeded
1 lime, peeled and seeded
1 tablespoon sunflower seeds
2 cups coconut water

1. Combine all ingredients and blend on high until smooth.
2. Add more liquid if necessary.

NUTRITIONAL INFORMATION (PER SERVING SIZE):

CALORIES:	FAT:	PROTEIN:	SODIUM:	CARBOHYDRATES:	SUGAR:	FIBER:
95	1.5 grams	2.3 grams	41 milligrams	21.0 grams	14.8 grams	4.4 grams

Cavegirl Coffee Smoothie

A large number of people in the Paleo community have been enjoying the flavor and health benefits of adding real butter (yep, that's right) to their coffee mugs in the morning. If dairy really bothers your gut health, use ghee, which is void of milk solids; however, a little bit of real butter from grass-fed cows is considered healthy if your system is not bothered by dairy. This creamy green concoction plays on that trend. It will give you a proper caffeine jolt, keep your tummy filled and satisfied, and have your taste buds coming back for more.

Recipe Yields: 3–4 cups

2 cups Bibb or Boston lettuce
2 frozen and peeled bananas
1 tablespoon pure, organic butter from grass-fed cows
1 tablespoon coconut oil
½ teaspoon vanilla or seeds from ½ vanilla bean
2 cups black coffee, chilled

1. Combine all ingredients and blend on high until smooth.
2. Add more liquid if necessary.

NUTRITIONAL INFORMATION (PER SERVING SIZE):

CALORIES:	FAT:	PROTEIN:	SODIUM:	CARBOHYDRATES:	SUGAR:	FIBER:
115	6.4 grams	1.2 grams	14 milligrams	14.2 grams	7.5 grams	1.8 grams

Bananalicious Smoothie

Before adding them to your smoothie, soaking nuts and seeds overnight helps wash away the naturally occurring anti-nutrients such as phytic acid and tannins. It also increases the potency of vitamins and helps with the growth of healthy enzymes necessary for healthy digestion. Soaking is not necessary; however, to get the most from seeds and nuts, you may want to take this extra step.

Recipe Yields: 3–4 cups

2 cups butter lettuce
2 peeled and frozen bananas
1 medium apple of choice, peeled and cored
1 tablespoon sunflower seeds
6 pecan halves
2 cups water

1. Combine all ingredients and blend on high until smooth.
2. Add more liquid if necessary.

NUTRITIONAL INFORMATION (PER SERVING SIZE):

CALORIES:	FAT:	PROTEIN:	SODIUM:	CARBOHYDRATES:	SUGAR:	FIBER:
103	2.9 grams	1.7 grams	6 milligrams	20.0 grams	11.6 grams	2.8 grams

Last Mango in Paris Smoothie

The coconut water in this smoothie is full of electrolytes. Read your labels—you want water straight from a young coconut with no added sugars, flavors, or chemicals. If you're drinking this smoothie post-workout, you may want to add a small spoonful of almond butter or a raw pastured egg to the blender for a punch of protein.

Recipe Yields: 3–4 cups

2 cups dandelion greens
1 cup frozen mango cubes
½ cup frozen pineapple cubes
½ cup strawberries, stems removed
2 cups coconut water

1. Combine all ingredients and blend on high until smooth.
2. Add more liquid if necessary.

NUTRITIONAL INFORMATION (PER SERVING SIZE):

CALORIES:	FAT:	PROTEIN:	SODIUM:	CARBOHYDRATES:	SUGAR:	FIBER:
81	0.2 gram	1.3 grams	52 milligrams	20.1 grams	13.4 grams	2.3 grams

Wake Up and Smell the Grapefruit Smoothie

Grapefruit and cucumber combine in this smoothie to offer a refreshing zing to your morning. It provides lots of vitamins and nutrients that will wake you up and keep you feeling fresh throughout the day. Although the grapefruit is known for being rich in vitamin C, this citrus fruit has been used for building immunity and for treating symptoms of illness such as common colds and bone disorders. The next time you start feeling feverish, the best thing to take may be a healthy helping of this grapefruit smoothie.

Recipe Yields: 3–4 cups

2 cups baby greens
2 small pears of choice, peeled and cored
1 cucumber, peeled and sliced
Juice from 2 red grapefruits
¼ cup water
2 teaspoons raw honey, optional

1. Combine all ingredients and blend on high until smooth.
2. Add more liquid if necessary.

NUTRITIONAL INFORMATION (PER SERVING SIZE): (WITHOUT HONEY)

CALORIES:	FAT:	PROTEIN:	SODIUM:	CARBOHYDRATES:	SUGAR:	FIBER:
88	0.2 gram	1.1 grams	18 milligrams	23.3 grams	8.7 grams	3.0 grams

Carrot Top Smoothie

Rich in beta-carotene, this smoothie blends romaine lettuce with tasty carrots and mango to give you a sweet start that can help you stay focused, gain lasting energy, and maintain the health of your eyes and metabolism. Don't forget to wash and use the greens on top of those organic carrots. They are full of nutrition too.

Recipe Yields: 3–4 cups

2 cups romaine lettuce
3 medium carrots and their top greens, peeled
1 mango, peeled and pitted
Juice of 2 oranges
1 cup water

1. Combine all ingredients and blend on high until smooth.
2. Add more liquid if necessary.

NUTRITIONAL INFORMATION (PER SERVING SIZE):

CALORIES:	FAT:	PROTEIN:	SODIUM:	CARBOHYDRATES:	SUGAR:	FIBER:
85	0.2 gram	0.9 gram	35 milligrams	21.5 grams	16.6 grams	3.0 grams

Strawberry Wake-Up Call Smoothie

Medjools, the king of dates, liven up this smoothie not only with the fruit's natural sweetness, but also with the nutritional benefits of protein, potassium, and copper. Because Medjool dates are fiber-rich, this smoothie will stick with you and help curtail sweet cravings if you have a sugar addiction or a break room at work full of doughnuts.

Recipe Yields: 3–4 cups

2 cups spinach
3 cups frozen strawberries, stems removed
2 Medjool dates, pitted and chopped
2 cups unsweetened almond milk

1. Combine all ingredients and blend on high until smooth.
2. Add more liquid if necessary.

NUTRITIONAL INFORMATION (PER SERVING SIZE):

CALORIES:	FAT:	PROTEIN:	SODIUM:	CARBOHYDRATES:	SUGAR:	FIBER:
90	1.4 grams	1.6 grams	93 milligrams	19.7 grams	13.1 grams	3.5 grams

Sunrise Smoothie

Full of citrus fruits, this smoothie screams "good morning." Enjoy this with a hard-boiled egg on your way to work and you won't be tempted to hit a drive-thru for breakfast. In addition, you will have strong resolve to fight off any coworkers bearing well-intended muffins.

Recipe Yields: 3–4 cups

2 cups green leaf lettuce
2 celery stalks with leaves
1 cup frozen pineapple cubes
1 orange, peeled and seeded
Juice of 1 grapefruit
1 cup water
1–2 teaspoons raw honey, optional

1. Combine all ingredients and blend on high until smooth.
2. Add more liquid if necessary.

NUTRITIONAL INFORMATION (PER SERVING SIZE): (WITHOUT HONEY)

CALORIES:	FAT:	PROTEIN:	SODIUM:	CARBOHYDRATES:	SUGAR:	FIBER:
63	0.1 gram	1.2 grams	23 milligrams	15.7 grams	4.6 grams	2.1 grams

Pucker Up Smoothie

The tartness of lemons and limes is balanced by crisp kale and raw honey in this smoothie. Coconut milk adds a natural fat that aids in weight loss and a beautiful complexion. Not only do lemons and limes have the acidity and tang to make you pucker up; they are incredibly healthy, too. Those same small, sour fruits that can bring a tear to your eye promote a balanced alkaline level in your body.

Recipe Yields: 3–4 cups

2 cups baby kale
2 lemons, peeled and seeded
2 limes, peeled and seeded
½ avocado, pitted and skin removed
2 tablespoons raw honey
2 cups coconut milk
3 coconut water ice cubes

1. Combine all ingredients and blend on high until smooth.
2. Add more liquid if necessary.

NUTRITIONAL INFORMATION (PER SERVING SIZE):

CALORIES:	FAT:	PROTEIN:	SODIUM:	CARBOHYDRATES:	SUGAR:	FIBER:
343	27.1 grams	3.6 grams	26 milligrams	21.2 grams	11.0 grams	3.3 grams

The Green Go-Getter Smoothie

Packed with green spinach and apples, this creamy green smoothie will kick off your morning with a boost of essential amino acids, vitamins, minerals, and an absolutely amazing taste. The combination of bananas, apples, and spinach—with more fruit than greens—provides an appetizing, sweeter taste and lessens the intensity of the spinach. This smoothie is a great one to start with if you're turned off by the strong, somewhat bitter taste of greens.

Recipe Yields: 3–4 cups

2 cups baby spinach
2 medium green apples, peeled and cored
1 peeled and frozen banana
¼ teaspoon cinnamon
2 cups green tea, cooled

1. Combine all ingredients and blend on high until smooth.
2. Add more liquid if necessary.

NUTRITIONAL INFORMATION (PER SERVING SIZE):

CALORIES:	FAT:	PROTEIN:	SODIUM:	CARBOHYDRATES:	SUGAR:	FIBER:
69	0.1 gram	1.0 gram	13 milligrams	17.9 grams	11.8 grams	2.2 grams

Kooky Kiwi Smoothie

Oranges aren't the only way to get vitamin C in the morning. Kiwis are an excellent source and help guard against infections and free radicals. In addition, they are heart-healthy, blood pressure–regulating, bone-strengthening power fruits. Best of all, they are tasty, especially when paired with the complimentary sweet cantaloupe in this smoothie.

Recipe Yields: 3–4 cups

2 cups green leaf lettuce
4 kiwis, peeled
1 cup cantaloupe
¼ cup pumpkin seeds
2 cups coconut water

1. Combine all ingredients and blend on high until smooth.
2. Add more liquid if necessary.

NUTRITIONAL INFORMATION (PER SERVING SIZE):

CALORIES:	FAT:	PROTEIN:	SODIUM:	CARBOHYDRATES:	SUGAR:	FIBER:
122	3.6 grams	3.8 grams	46 milligrams	20.1 grams	14.3 grams	3.1 grams

Crack of Dawn Smoothie

Don't be afraid to crack an egg or two in your smoothies. Choose pastured eggs from free-range hens, and wash the exterior shell prior to cracking to remove bacteria. Avoid commercial eggs that come from caged hens and have been contaminated with feces and dirt. An egg offers perfect protein and is so much better than the factory-made protein powders available. In addition, an egg gives a fluffiness to the smoothie that no other ingredient achieves.

Recipe Yields: 3–4 cups

2 cups spinach
2 large pastured eggs
1 cup frozen seedless green grapes
1 cup strawberries, stems removed
2 cups unsweetened almond milk

1. Combine all ingredients and blend on high until smooth.
2. Add more liquid if necessary.

NUTRITIONAL INFORMATION (PER SERVING SIZE):

CALORIES:	FAT:	PROTEIN:	SODIUM:	CARBOHYDRATES:	SUGAR:	FIBER:
85	3.4 grams	4.4 grams	127 milligrams	10.6 grams	7.7 grams	1.4 grams

CHAPTER 5
Everyday Smoothies

Incorporating green smoothies into your Paleo lifestyle can have lasting beneficial effects. Think of it as a little healthful injection of nutrition . . . a present to yourself in the midst of the craziness of the daily grind. Change up your greens, try weird fruits, and experiment with new vegetables. Variety is the spice of life, and this cliché couldn't be truer when it comes to produce. Each fruit or veggie has its own unique blend of phytochemicals that your body needs. Feeling a little rowdy? Try a Kale Yeah Smoothie and scream out the name . . . it's a little silly, but kind of fun too. When you want to relax at the end of a hard day, try the Mojito Smoothie and let the flavors take your imagination to the beach. Just be mindful of your life and savor every second.

Kale Yeah Smoothie

The sweetness from the beet and banana in this smoothie masks the bitterness of the kale. The oranges give it a little citrus zip. Cheers to your health with this rockin' combination full of potassium, magnesium, fiber, vitamins, and so much more. This smoothie will have you yelling, "Kale Yeah!"

Recipe Yields: 3–4 cups

2 cups kale
½ beet, peeled and diced
½ peeled and frozen banana
2 oranges, peeled and seeded
2 cups green tea, cooled

1. Combine all ingredients and blend on high until smooth.
2. Add more liquid if necessary.

NUTRITIONAL INFORMATION (PER SERVING SIZE):

CALORIES:	FAT:	PROTEIN:	SODIUM:	CARBOHYDRATES:	SUGAR:	FIBER:
54	0.1 gram	1.2 grams	11 milligrams	13.4 grams	9.1 grams	2.7 grams

Taxi Mom Smoothie

This smoothie is packed with happy yellow produce to give you a boost while driving your "mom taxi" around town. By providing you with high levels of potassium, this guilt-free drink encourages proper muscle and nerve function. And with a carful of kidlets, your nerves may need all the help they can get.

Recipe Yields: 3–4 cups

2 cups mixed greens
½ yellow bell pepper, seeded
½ cup frozen pineapple chunks
½ peeled and frozen banana
½ lemon, peeled and seeded
1 tablespoon sunflower seeds
2 cups green tea, cooled

1. Combine all ingredients and blend on high until smooth.
2. Add more liquid if necessary.

NUTRITIONAL INFORMATION (PER SERVING SIZE):

CALORIES:	FAT:	PROTEIN:	SODIUM:	CARBOHYDRATES:	SUGAR:	FIBER:
46	1.2 grams	1.3 grams	17 milligrams	9.9 grams	2.5 grams	1.6 grams

Berry Green Smoothie

Don't let the dandelion greens scare you away from making this tropical delight . . . you can always substitute arugula, spinach, or whatever greens you have in your refrigerator. However, dandelion greens are high in fiber and work as a laxative as well as touting the benefit of reducing cholesterol in the blood. Also high in carotenes, they help protect against lung and oral cancers.

Recipe Yields: 3–4 cups

2 cups dandelion greens
½ cup unsweetened coconut flakes
2 cups frozen blackberries
1 medium carrot, peeled
2 cups coconut water

1. Combine all ingredients and blend on high until smooth.
2. Add more liquid if necessary.

NUTRITIONAL INFORMATION (PER SERVING SIZE):

CALORIES:	FAT:	PROTEIN:	SODIUM:	CARBOHYDRATES:	SUGAR:	FIBER:
138	5.4 grams	2.5 grams	66 milligrams	23.0 grams	14.3 grams	6.1 grams

Coco-Nana Smoothie

This straightforward, quick-and-good smoothie is a great "starter" smoothie, as the mellow coconut and banana flavors do a great job of masking the sharpness of the greens. The nutmeg not only adds a nice touch of spice; it brings with it a long list of nutritional benefits including boosting skin health, reducing insomnia, managing diabetes, and improving blood circulation.

Recipe Yields: 3–4 cups

2 cups baby spinach
½ cup unsweetened coconut flakes
2 peeled and frozen bananas
¼ teaspoon ground nutmeg
2 cups coconut water

1. Combine all ingredients and blend on high until smooth.
2. Add more liquid if necessary.

NUTRITIONAL INFORMATION (PER SERVING SIZE):

CALORIES:	FAT:	PROTEIN:	SODIUM:	CARBOHYDRATES:	SUGAR:	FIBER:
128	5.2 grams	1.9 grams	46 milligrams	21.3 grams	12.6 grams	2.9 grams

Ginger-Citrus Stress Away Smoothie

The tang of citrus from the pineapple and the zing of ginger make for a stimulating blend that will put your senses and taste buds on high alert. Delicious and rejuvenating, this zippy treat can instantly turn around a stressful day. Buy whole flax seeds and grind them just before using, otherwise they can go rancid pretty quickly.

Recipe Yields: 3–4 cups

2 cups watercress
2 cups frozen pineapple chunks
1 peeled and frozen banana
½" knob ginger, peeled
1 tablespoon flax seeds
2 cups green tea, cooled

1. Combine all ingredients and blend on high until smooth.
2. Add more liquid if necessary.

NUTRITIONAL INFORMATION (PER SERVING SIZE):

CALORIES:	FAT:	PROTEIN:	SODIUM:	CARBOHYDRATES:	SUGAR:	FIBER:
89	1.2 grams	1.7 grams	8 milligrams	20.0 grams	5.7 grams	2.9 grams

Give 'Em Hell Smoothie

You know those days. Sometimes you feel fired up. Well, the kick of cayenne in this drink will match your fire. Add more for intensity if you can handle it! Drink this flavorful combination and enjoy all the added health benefits found in every ingredient in this powerful recipe.

Recipe Yields: 3–4 cups

2 cups spinach
2 peeled and frozen bananas
½ teaspoon cayenne pepper
1 tablespoon unsweetened cocoa powder
1 teaspoon ground cinnamon
1 tablespoon raw honey
2 cups unsweetened almond milk

1. Combine all ingredients and blend on high until smooth.
2. Add more liquid if necessary.

NUTRITIONAL INFORMATION (PER SERVING SIZE):

CALORIES:	FAT:	PROTEIN:	SODIUM:	CARBOHYDRATES:	SUGAR:	FIBER:
91	1.6 grams	1.9 grams	92 milligrams	19.8 grams	11.7 grams	2.8 grams

Over the Top Smoothie

The tops of vegetables are often tossed away with the weekly trash. But did you know that many contain beneficial nutrients and are completely edible? Not only are they edible, but they are delicious. In addition to putting them in a smoothie, you can chop the top greens and add them to salads, soups, and even sauté them for a beautiful side dish.

Recipe Yields: 3–4 cups

1 cup watercress
½ beet plus greens, peeled and chopped
1 celery stalk, plus leaves
1 small carrot, plus top greens
4 Brazil nuts
2 cups green tea, cooled

1. Combine all ingredients and blend on high until smooth.
2. Add more liquid if necessary.

NUTRITIONAL INFORMATION (PER SERVING SIZE):

CALORIES:	FAT:	PROTEIN:	SODIUM:	CARBOHYDRATES:	SUGAR:	FIBER:
45	3.1 grams	1.3 grams	39 milligrams	3.9 grams	1.8 grams	1.4 grams

Mojito Smoothie

Although you can certainly add the real thing to this smoothie, rum—and most alcohol—is considered a no-no in the Paleo community due to the high sugar content and toxicity caused to the liver. However, there are times when some people make exceptions and let their hair down. If you use the extract, note that imitation versions are filled with artificial ingredients. Use the natural varieties for a more complex flavor.

Recipe Yields: 3–4 cups

1½ cups Bibb or Boston lettuce
½ cup fresh mint
4 limes, peeled and seeded
4 Medjool dates, pitted and seeded
2 cups water
2 teaspoons rum extract, optional

1. Combine all ingredients and blend on high until smooth.
2. Add more liquid if necessary.

NUTRITIONAL INFORMATION (PER SERVING SIZE): (WITHOUT RUM EXTRACT)

CALORIES:	FAT:	PROTEIN:	SODIUM:	CARBOHYDRATES:	SUGAR:	FIBER:
43	0.1 gram	1.0 gram	7 milligrams	13.3 grams	6.0 grams	2.8 grams

Kombucha-Cha Smoothie

Kombucha is a fermented tea thought for thousands of years to be a healing tonic. It is popular within the Paleo community because it is another fermented food option. Sauerkraut, kimchi, kombucha, and other fermented foods help the digestive system, which is very important for gut health. Because kombucha has a strong and distinct flavor, "hiding" it in a smoothie may be the perfect way for someone who is at first put off by the drink.

Recipe Yields: 3–4 cups

2 cups spinach
2 cups frozen strawberries, stems removed
¼ cup unsweetened coconut flakes
1 teaspoon coconut oil
2 cups kombucha
1 tablespoon raw honey, optional

1. Combine all ingredients and blend on high until smooth.
2. Add more liquid if necessary.

NUTRITIONAL INFORMATION (PER SERVING SIZE): (WITHOUT HONEY)

CALORIES:	FAT:	PROTEIN:	SODIUM:	CARBOHYDRATES:	SUGAR:	FIBER:
78	3.6 grams	1.0 gram	19 milligrams	11.9 grams	4.7 grams	2.4 grams

Swiss Minty Smoothie

Swiss chard is actually in the beet family of vegetables and is very popular in Mediterranean regions. Loaded with phytonutrients, Swiss chard, when included regularly in diets, helps prevent osteoporosis and anemia. With the fresh flavor of mint, the hydrating nature of the cucumber, and the creaminess of the blended pear, this smoothie is sure to please.

Recipe Yields: 3–4 cups

1½ cups Swiss chard
½ cup fresh mint
2 cucumbers, peeled
2 medium pears of choice, peeled and cored
2 cups coconut water

1. Combine all ingredients and blend on high until smooth.
2. Add more liquid if necessary.

NUTRITIONAL INFORMATION (PER SERVING SIZE):

CALORIES:	FAT:	PROTEIN:	SODIUM:	CARBOHYDRATES:	SUGAR:	FIBER:
93	0.2 gram	1.8 grams	64 milligrams	22.8 grams	15.6 grams	4.2 grams

Trail Mix Smoothie

Ingest your trail mix in liquid form before your hike with this delicious smoothie. It will yield lasting energy while you maneuver your way through the forest, rocks, and water. For long hikes, freeze this drink in a portable bottle so that it will be melted and chilled by the time you are ready to take a break for an energy boost.

Recipe Yields: 3–4 cups

2 cups spinach
¼ cup unsweetened coconut flakes
1 medium apple of choice, peeled and cored
¼ cup goji berries
1 tablespoon unsweetened cocoa powder
4 pecan halves
1 tablespoon raw sunflower seeds
2 Medjool dates, pitted and diced
2 cups unsweetened almond milk

1. Combine all ingredients and blend on high until smooth.
2. Add more liquid if necessary.

NUTRITIONAL INFORMATION (PER SERVING SIZE):

CALORIES:	FAT:	PROTEIN:	SODIUM:	CARBOHYDRATES:	SUGAR:	FIBER:
121	6.2 grams	3.1 grams	112 milligrams	16.7 grams	7.8 grams	5.5 grams

Summer Love Smoothie

Yum . . . watermelon and strawberries! This smoothie makes you think of summer and cook-outs and fun. Keep your guests happy and hydrated with this delicious and nutritious cocktail. If you want it more on the slushy side, freeze coconut water in an ice tray the night before. Add the cubes to the recipe below. This gives you iciness without watering down your drink.

Recipe Yields: 3–4 cups

2 cups spinach
6 mint leaves
1 cup watermelon cubes
1 cup frozen strawberries, stems removed
½ avocado, peeled and pitted
2 cups coconut water

1. Combine all ingredients and blend on high until smooth.
2. Add more liquid if necessary.

NUTRITIONAL INFORMATION (PER SERVING SIZE):

CALORIES:	FAT:	PROTEIN:	SODIUM:	CARBOHYDRATES:	SUGAR:	FIBER:
80	2.7 grams	1.5 grams	45 milligrams	13.6 grams	9.0 grams	2.5 grams

Terrific Turmeric Smoothie

Turmeric is a yellow root herbaceous plant that belongs to the ginger family. When you ingest it, your body absorbs its nutrients slowly so you get ample benefits. One way to assist with this is to consume it with oil, such as the coconut oil in this smoothie. The coconut oil not only assists the turmeric's nutritional absorption; it is great for digestion. Topically, coconut oil is also an excellent option for your complexion.

Recipe Yields: 3–4 cups

2 cups green leaf lettuce
1½ cups frozen mango cubes
½ cup mixed berries
1 teaspoon coconut oil
½" knob turmeric, peeled or ¼ teaspoon dried turmeric
2 cups green tea, cooled

1. Combine all ingredients and blend on high until smooth.
2. Add more liquid if necessary.

NUTRITIONAL INFORMATION (PER SERVING SIZE):

CALORIES:	FAT:	PROTEIN:	SODIUM:	CARBOHYDRATES:	SUGAR:	FIBER:
66	1.1 grams	0.4 gram	6 milligrams	14.9 grams	11.8 grams	1.9 grams

Almond Mocha Smoothie

Bananas are not only a fantastic source of potassium; they are a great thickening agent for smoothies and give a creamy texture to your drink. Peel your bananas before freezing them. Otherwise the peel freezes to the fruit and it is difficult to work with if you are counting on a quick meal to go.

Recipe Yields: 3–4 cups

2 cups romaine lettuce
2 peeled and frozen bananas
1 tablespoon unsweetened cocoa powder
1 tablespoon sunflower seeds
6 almonds
1 cup unsweetened almond milk
1 cup black coffee, cooled

1. Combine all ingredients and blend on high until smooth.
2. Add more liquid if necessary.

NUTRITIONAL INFORMATION (PER SERVING SIZE):

CALORIES:	FAT:	PROTEIN:	SODIUM:	CARBOHYDRATES:	SUGAR:	FIBER:
90	3.0 grams	2.3 grams	43 milligrams	15.8 grams	7.6 grams	3.0 grams

CHAPTER 6
Savory Smoothies

If you're not used to smoothies, savory smoothies can be hard drinks to start with because they don't hit that happy sweet place that we often expect from something made in a blender. Ease into smoothies by starting with ones found in some of the other chapters of this book, and then slowly add more veggies and less fruit to accommodate your taste buds. The Broccoli-Bok Choy Smoothie is a nice Asian-inspired drink that may grow into your new favorite! If you choose to indulge on your cheat days or the weekends with a shot of alcohol in your drinks, the smoothies in this chapter will be a great fit. You may want to try adding tequila, especially to the Tomatillo Mary Smoothie. But if you choose to imbibe, choose the good stuff. According to Dr. Loren Cordain, nutrition expert and founder of the Paleo Diet movement, buy tequila distilled 100 percent from agave plants with no added sugars.

Cabbage-Carrot Smoothie

It turns out that putting some rabbit food into your own diet can have healthy benefits. The humble cabbage is a member of the cruciferous veggie family and has been used to treat arthritis, scurvy, obesity, eczema, and a slew of other ailments. It also adds a subtle spiciness to the smoothie.

Recipe Yields: 3–4 cups

2 cups green cabbage
3 carrots, peeled
1 medium tart apple, peeled and cored
2 celery stalks, with leaves
1" knob ginger, peeled
2 cups water

1. Combine all ingredients and blend on high until smooth.
2. Add more liquid if necessary.

NUTRITIONAL INFORMATION (PER SERVING SIZE):

CALORIES:	FAT:	PROTEIN:	SODIUM:	CARBOHYDRATES:	SUGAR:	FIBER:
52	0.1 gram	1.3 grams	60 milligrams	12.8 grams	7.9 grams	3.3 grams

Tomatillo Mary Smoothie

The tomatillos in this Bloody Mary alternative are loaded with nutritional benefits to aid in weight loss, improve digestion, help prevent some cancers, and increase energy levels, to name a few. The jalapeño provides a little kick in the middle of the afternoon as well as vitamins A and C, phenols, flavonoids, and capsaicinoids that help the body fight inflammation.

Recipe Yields: 3–4 cups

2 cups spinach
1 tablespoon cilantro
3 tomatillos, husked and cored
1 green onion
½ lime, peeled and seeded
1 cucumber, peeled
½ jalapeño (keep seeds for extra heat)
Pinch of sea salt
2 cups water

1. Combine all ingredients and blend on high until smooth.
2. Add more liquid if necessary.

NUTRITIONAL INFORMATION (PER SERVING SIZE):

CALORIES:	FAT:	PROTEIN:	SODIUM:	CARBOHYDRATES:	SUGAR:	FIBER:
23	0.2 gram	1.2 grams	42 milligrams	4.8 grams	2.3 grams	1.7 grams

Summer Squash Smoothie

Summer squash is one of the easiest squash to grow even for the not-so-green-thumb person. This smoothie is a tasty and healthy way to use some of your garden's yield. High in manganese, summer squash can help with women's monthly mood swings and cramps, so drink up and soothe your aches.

Recipe Yields: 3–4 cups

2 cups baby kale
1–2 sprigs parsley
2 summer squash, diced
2 small pears of choice, peeled and cored
1 parsnip, peeled
1 garlic clove
2 cups white tea, cooled

1. Combine all ingredients and blend on high until smooth.
2. Add more liquid if necessary.

NUTRITIONAL INFORMATION (PER SERVING SIZE):

CALORIES:	FAT:	PROTEIN:	SODIUM:	CARBOHYDRATES:	SUGAR:	FIBER:
99	0.4 gram	2.5 grams	9 milligrams	24.7 grams	13.0 grams	5.6 grams

Asparagus-Avocado Smoothie

Avocado really is nature's little miracle. It gives whatever it's added to a creamy and luxurious texture. Not only high in vitamins A, K, D, and E, avocados have proven to help with the absorption of other nutrients so they raise the nutritional value of other veggies and fruits around them . . . like when you use one in a smoothie.

Recipe Yields: 3–4 cups

1 cup mixed greens
2 cups chopped asparagus, tough ends discarded
½ avocado, peeled and pitted
1 celery stalk, including leaves
1 small tart apple, peeled and cored
Juice from ½ lime
Pinch of sea salt
2 cups green tea, cooled

1. Combine all ingredients and blend on high until smooth.
2. Add more liquid if necessary.

NUTRITIONAL INFORMATION (PER SERVING SIZE):

CALORIES:	FAT:	PROTEIN:	SODIUM:	CARBOHYDRATES:	SUGAR:	FIBER:
63	2.7 grams	2.1 grams	53 milligrams	9.7 grams	4.9 grams	3.4 grams

Broccoli-Bok Choy Smoothie

This Asian-inspired smoothie gets a nutritional boost from the addition of a small amount of coconut aminos. Coconut aminos are a soy sauce substitute that is soy-free, gluten-free, and dairy-free and can be found in most specialty stores, natural food stores, and online. Made from raw coconut sap, they have a notable amount of amino acids, which contribute to the repair of muscle tissue. So, drink up after an active day and let your body heal itself while you relax.

Recipe Yields: 3–4 cups

1 cup chopped bok choy
1 cup chopped broccoli
1 celery stalk, including leaves
1 teaspoon coconut aminos
⅛ teaspoon Chinese five-spice powder
1 garlic clove
2 teaspoons sesame seeds
Pinch of sea salt
2 cups green tea, cooled

1. Combine all ingredients and blend on high until smooth.
2. Add more liquid if necessary.

NUTRITIONAL INFORMATION (PER SERVING SIZE):

CALORIES:	FAT:	PROTEIN:	SODIUM:	CARBOHYDRATES:	SUGAR:	FIBER:
19	0.8 gram	1.1 grams	81 milligrams	2.6 grams	0.2 gram	0.5 gram

Fennel-Cucumber Smoothie

Pairing fennel, which is high in vitamin C, and spinach, which is high in iron, will help maximize your body's absorption of iron. If you are suffering from anemia, this smoothie will aid in transporting oxygen to your tissues, which will result in higher energy levels.

Recipe Yields: 3–4 cups

1 cup spinach
1 fennel bulb, including fronds (strip these
**   from the tough, yet edible, stalks)**
½ cucumber, peeled
1 celery stalk, including leaves
1 medium carrot, peeled
Pinch of sea salt
2 cups water

1. Combine all ingredients and blend on high until smooth.
2. Add more liquid if necessary.

NUTRITIONAL INFORMATION (PER SERVING SIZE):

CALORIES:	FAT:	PROTEIN:	SODIUM:	CARBOHYDRATES:	SUGAR:	FIBER:
31	0.3 gram	1.4 grams	93 milligrams	7.1 grams	3.7 grams	2.8 grams

Zesty Zucchini Smoothie

Fresh horseradish gives this smoothie the zest that it deserves. Your sinuses will thank you immediately. Horseradish has been used in many cultures around the world to boost immune systems due to the vitamins and phytochemicals present in the root. For the full experience, enjoy this smoothie on the back porch with a plate of freshly shucked oysters!

Recipe Yields: 3–4 cups

2 cups chopped collard greens
2 small zucchinis
½ cucumber, peeled
1 carrot, peeled
1 Roma tomato
2 teaspoons freshly grated horseradish
2 cups water

1. Combine all ingredients and blend on high until smooth.
2. Add more liquid if necessary.

NUTRITIONAL INFORMATION (PER SERVING SIZE):

CALORIES:	FAT:	PROTEIN:	SODIUM:	CARBOHYDRATES:	SUGAR:	FIBER:
42	0.6 gram	2.4 grams	38 milligrams	8.2 grams	5.4 grams	2.7 grams

Spinach-Cilantro Smoothie

Forget the water in this smoothie—add a little avocado and serve this right out of the blender on some tortilla chips . . . Paleo tortilla chips that is, made from cassava flour. However you decide to enjoy it, know that you are doing great things for your body with these fresh, organic foods.

Recipe Yields: 3–4 cups

2 cups spinach
¼ cup cilantro leaves
1 Roma tomato
2 celery stalks, including leaves
1 garlic clove
½ lime, peeled and seeded
2 cups water

1. Combine all ingredients and blend on high until smooth.
2. Add more liquid if necessary.

NUTRITIONAL INFORMATION (PER SERVING SIZE):

CALORIES:	FAT:	PROTEIN:	SODIUM:	CARBOHYDRATES:	SUGAR:	FIBER:
18	0.3 gram	0.9 gram	33 milligrams	4.1 grams	2.0 grams	1.2 grams

Peppery Tomato Smoothie

With its strong peppery flavor, arugula usually has to be "hidden" in smoothies, but in this recipe, the other ingredients gather around it and celebrate its unique flavor. If you like your smoothies spicy, substitute a jalapeño for the onion. Get creative and have fun finding the exact combination for your taste preference.

Recipe Yields: 3–4 cups

2 cups arugula
3 medium beefsteak tomatoes
2 medium carrots, peeled
¼ red onion, diced
½ lime, peeled and seeded
2 cups water

1. Combine all ingredients and blend on high until smooth.
2. Add more liquid if necessary.

NUTRITIONAL INFORMATION (PER SERVING SIZE):

CALORIES:	FAT:	PROTEIN:	SODIUM:	CARBOHYDRATES:	SUGAR:	FIBER:
36	0.2 gram	1.5 grams	32 milligrams	8.4 grams	4.5 grams	2.3 grams

Turnip the Beet Smoothie

Turn up the beat and dance away while drinking this root veggie smoothie. When purchasing turnips, choose the smaller ones as they have a sweeter taste. Loaded with fiber, vitamins, and minerals, this filling drink will surprise you with its creamy texture and will curb your appetite and cravings.

Recipe Yields: 3–4 cups

1 small turnip plus greens, peeled and diced
1 small beet plus beet greens, peeled and diced
2 medium tart apples, peeled and cored
½ lemon, peeled and seeded
2 cups water

1. Combine all ingredients and blend on high until smooth.
2. Add more liquid if necessary.

NUTRITIONAL INFORMATION (PER SERVING SIZE):

CALORIES:	FAT:	PROTEIN:	SODIUM:	CARBOHYDRATES:	SUGAR:	FIBER:
55	0.1 gram	0.9 gram	36 milligrams	14.2 grams	10.3 grams	2.3 grams

Ahoy Savoy Smoothie

You can buy sesame seeds already toasted in the spice aisle in most grocery stores, but if you can only find them plain, no worries. Using an ungreased skillet, cook the seeds over medium heat for about 3–4 minutes, pushing these little high-quality protein gems around until they are lightly browned.

Recipe Yields: 3–4 cups

2 cups savoy cabbage
1 peeled and frozen banana
½ avocado, peeled and pitted
1 cup frozen pineapple cubes
1 tablespoon toasted sesame seeds
2 cups coconut water

1. Combine all ingredients and blend on high until smooth.
2. Add more liquid if necessary.

NUTRITIONAL INFORMATION (PER SERVING SIZE):

CALORIES:	FAT:	PROTEIN:	SODIUM:	CARBOHYDRATES:	SUGAR:	FIBER:
124	3.7 grams	2.4 grams	43 milligrams	22.3 grams	10.3 grams	4.1 grams

Why Not Cauliflower Smoothie

Cauliflower is not the first thing that comes to mind when choosing ingredients for a smoothie. However, why not try it? Cauliflower provides allicin, an important compound that reduces the risk of stroke and heart disease while detoxifying the blood and liver. With abilities like that, this veggie is a must-have in any disease-preventing diet.

Recipe Yields: 3–4 cups

**2 cups romaine lettuce
1 cup chopped cauliflower
2 carrots, peeled
1 small apple of choice, peeled and cored
1 tablespoon pumpkin seeds
2 cups water**

1. Combine all ingredients and blend on high until smooth.
2. Add more liquid if necessary.

NUTRITIONAL INFORMATION (PER SERVING SIZE):

CALORIES:	FAT:	PROTEIN:	SODIUM:	CARBOHYDRATES:	SUGAR:	FIBER:
49	1.0 gram	1.73 grams	35 milligrams	9.5 grams	5.6 grams	2.4 grams

Indian Cuminty Smoothie

Fresh herbs are easy to grow in a small garden or containers—you can even have an herb garden right in your kitchen. But a word of warning about mint: It grows like weeds. Plant mint in a container instead of directly in the ground. Left unattended, mint will take over your yard!

Recipe Yields: 3–4 cups

2 cups arugula
¼ cup mint leaves
3 cucumbers, peeled
1 celery stalk, with leaves
½ lime, peeled and seeded
½ teaspoon ground cumin
¼ teaspoon ground ginger (or a small knob fresh ginger)
2 cups water

1. Combine all ingredients and blend on high until smooth.
2. Add more liquid if necessary.

NUTRITIONAL INFORMATION (PER SERVING SIZE):

CALORIES:	FAT:	PROTEIN:	SODIUM:	CARBOHYDRATES:	SUGAR:	FIBER:
33	0.2 gram	1.7 grams	19 milligrams	6.5 grams	3.4 grams	2.2 grams

Spinach Power Smoothie

In addition to being a rich source of iron and folate (which aids in iron absorption), spinach holds a wealth of vitamins A, B, C, D, and K that provide cancer-fighting power against liver, ovarian, colon, and prostate cancers. By including just 1 cup of this mighty veggie in your daily diet (raw), you'll get over 180 percent of your daily need for vitamin K.

Recipe Yields: 3–4 cups

2 cups spinach
1 cucumber, peeled
2 celery stalks, with leaves
1 small tomato
½ cup frozen blueberries
2 cups green tea, cooled

1. Combine all ingredients and blend on high until smooth.
2. Add more liquid if necessary.

NUTRITIONAL INFORMATION (PER SERVING SIZE):

CALORIES:	FAT:	PROTEIN:	SODIUM:	CARBOHYDRATES:	SUGAR:	FIBER:
29	0.2 gram	1.3 grams	31 milligrams	6.1 grams	3.5 grams	1.9 grams

CHAPTER 7
Dessert Smoothies

Even among the strict Paleo police, I think this chapter is secretly their favorite. If not, it should be! Dessert smoothies take you back to the wonderful smells from the kitchen and bring up some happy childhood memories—especially the Not Your Grandma's Banana Nut Smoothie. The upside is that you won't find any gluten or refined sugar in these recipes. The bad stuff is replaced with nutritious produce and healthful ingredients, but you still are able to indulge a bit. Instead of getting that pumpkin frappe from you know where, save some money and calories and make your very own Pumpkin Pie Smoothie. It is a more satiating option and will see you through until your next meal. These drinks are sweeter with more natural sugars than other hardcore green smoothies in this book, so use your best judgment on how often you incorporate them into your daily life.

Chocolate Mint Smoothie

A crowd-pleaser, this is a beginner smoothie for the skeptics. It's perfect as a meal replacement, because the almond butter provides protein to round out the nutritional profile of this sweet treat.

Recipe Yields: 3–4 cups

1½ cups spinach
¼ cup mint leaves
2 peeled and frozen bananas
½ cup frozen seedless grapes
1 tablespoon unsweetened cocoa powder
2 tablespoons almond butter
1 cup unsweetened almond milk
1 cup peppermint tea, cooled

1. Combine all ingredients and blend on high until smooth.
2. Add more liquid if necessary.

NUTRITIONAL INFORMATION (PER SERVING SIZE):

CALORIES:	FAT:	PROTEIN:	SODIUM:	CARBOHYDRATES:	SUGAR:	FIBER:
128	5.0 grams	3.4 grams	50 milligrams	19.8 grams	10.6 grams	3.4 grams

Pumpkin Pie Smoothie

Yum . . . this creamy smoothie will make you think of Thanksgiving celebrations. The pure maple syrup is easier on the stomach than refined sugar, which can cause indigestion and gas. The pumpkin contains tryptophan, which is important in the production of serotonin. Serotonin is a mood enhancer and will help you handle the craziness of your family get-together.

Recipe Yields: 3–4 cups

2 cups mixed greens
1 peeled and frozen banana
¼ cup organic pumpkin purée
2 teaspoons cinnamon
2 teaspoons pumpkin pie spice
1 tablespoon pure maple syrup
2 tablespoons pumpkin seeds
2 cups unsweetened almond milk

1. Combine all ingredients and blend on high until smooth.
2. Add more liquid if necessary.

NUTRITIONAL INFORMATION (PER SERVING SIZE):

CALORIES:	FAT:	PROTEIN:	SODIUM:	CARBOHYDRATES:	SUGAR:	FIBER:
86	3.1 grams	2.5 grams	98 milligrams	14.1 grams	7.3 grams	2.7 grams

Not Your Grandma's Banana Nut Smoothie

Waking up to the sweet aroma of fresh-baked banana bread can't be replaced . . . until you taste this smoothie! When you think of antioxidant-rich foods, walnuts probably aren't your first thought, but just ¼ cup of walnuts carries almost 100 percent of your daily requirement for omega-3 fatty acids and is loaded with monounsaturated fats. Of the tree nuts, walnuts, chestnuts, and pecans carry the highest amount of antioxidants, which can prevent illness and reverse oxidative damage done by free radicals.

Recipe Yields: 3–4 cups

2 cups romaine lettuce
2 peeled and frozen bananas
1 small apple of choice, peeled and cored
1 teaspoon cinnamon
⅛ teaspoon nutmeg
¼ cup walnuts
2 teaspoons almond butter
2 cups unsweetened almond milk

1. Combine all ingredients and blend on high until smooth.
2. Add more liquid if necessary.

NUTRITIONAL INFORMATION (PER SERVING SIZE):

CALORIES:	FAT:	PROTEIN:	SODIUM:	CARBOHYDRATES:	SUGAR:	FIBER:
145	6.7 grams	3.1 grams	82 milligrams	20.4 grams	11.1 grams	3.5 grams

Just Peachy Green Smoothie

You'll feel like you're in Georgia enjoying this Southern delicacy made of peaches and pecans. And in the heat of the summer, this smoothie is perfect poured into popsicle molds and frozen to enjoy after a long run or just relaxing poolside with friends and family. Peaches can keep your skin healthy, reduce hair loss, and aid in the fight against obesity-related diabetes. So, dig in, y'all!

Recipe Yields: 3–4 cups

2 cups kale
4 mint leaves
2 cups frozen peach cubes
4 pecan halves
2 cups coconut milk

1. Combine all ingredients and blend on high until smooth.
2. Add more liquid if necessary.

NUTRITIONAL INFORMATION (PER SERVING SIZE):

CALORIES:	FAT:	PROTEIN:	SODIUM:	CARBOHYDRATES:	SUGAR:	FIBER:
245	23.7 grams	3.0 grams	17 milligrams	6.4 grams	1.9 grams	0.7 gram

Beet That Sweet Tooth Smoothie

When you're looking for a sweet treat, beets are vitamin- and nutrient-packed vegetables that offer up a sweet taste comparable to many fruits. This recipe is just one of the many greens-and-beet combinations that you'll enjoy. Both the root (the deep reddish-purple bulb we think of as the beet) and the greens of this nutritious, delicious little veggie are edible and highly nutritious. Packed with calcium, potassium, and vitamins A and C, these powerful veggies are a healthy addition to any diet.

Recipe Yields: 3–4 cups

2 cups beet greens
1 beet, peeled and diced
1 cup frozen mixed berries
½ peeled and frozen banana
2 cups unsweetened almond milk

1. Combine all ingredients and blend on high until smooth.
2. Add more liquid if necessary.

NUTRITIONAL INFORMATION (PER SERVING SIZE):

CALORIES:	FAT:	PROTEIN:	SODIUM:	CARBOHYDRATES:	SUGAR:	FIBER:
57	1.4 grams	1.6 grams	138 milligrams	10.4 grams	6.0 grams	2.8 grams

Key Lime Pie Smoothie

Good things come in small packages and this is definitely true of the key lime. The adorable citrus fruit packs a dynamic punch of flavor and vitamin C. You usually buy key limes in a netted bag, so if you have a lot left over, their strong acidic flavor and juicy nature lends itself well to a ceviche, which is a perfect summer Paleo meal.

Recipe Yields: 3–4 cups

2 cups iceberg lettuce
Zest and juice of 4 key limes
½ avocado, peeled and pitted
½ peeled and frozen banana
1 tablespoon raw honey
1 cup unsweetened almond milk
6 coconut water ice cubes
Almond meal, optional garnish

1. Combine all ingredients except almond meal and blend on high until smooth.
2. Add more liquid if necessary.
3. Sprinkle a little almond meal on top if desired to give it a "pie crust" texture.

NUTRITIONAL INFORMATION (PER SERVING SIZE): (WITHOUT ALMOND MEAL)

CALORIES:	FAT:	PROTEIN:	SODIUM:	CARBOHYDRATES:	SUGAR:	FIBER:
101	3.3 grams	1.5 grams	57 milligrams	18.3 grams	11.0 grams	2.6 grams

Piña Colada Smoothie

Jamaican me crazy with this traditional island concoction! Ice cubes can water down a smoothie once you blend it. Counter this problem by freezing coconut water in trays prior to making your drink. Pineapple is the star in this smoothie, both for taste and its high potassium content, which helps lower blood pressure.

Recipe Yields: 3–4 cups

2 cups spinach
2 cups frozen pineapple chunks
2 teaspoons rum extract (or the real deal
   if you are on a cheat day!)
2 cups coconut milk
8 coconut water ice cubes

1. Combine all ingredients and blend on high until smooth.
2. Add more liquid if necessary.

NUTRITIONAL INFORMATION (PER SERVING SIZE):

CALORIES:	FAT:	PROTEIN:	SODIUM:	CARBOHYDRATES:	SUGAR:	FIBER:
289	22.7 grams	3.5 grams	42 milligrams	18.6 grams	4.7 grams	1.7 grams

Mocha Delight Smoothie

Arugula, also known as rocket, is a member of the cruciferous veggie family, which includes broccoli and cauliflower. Although arugula is popular in salads, its peppery flavor doesn't lend itself to a lot of smoothies. However, the strong coffee flavor in this drink helps mask the intensity of the arugula, allowing you to still gain its health benefits.

Recipe Yields: 3–4 cups

2 cups arugula
1 tablespoon unsweetened cocoa
1 teaspoon raw honey
⅛ teaspoon cinnamon
1 peeled and frozen banana
½ cup unsweetened almond milk
1½ cups black coffee, cooled

1. Combine all ingredients and blend on high until smooth.
2. Add more liquid if necessary.

NUTRITIONAL INFORMATION (PER SERVING SIZE):

CALORIES:	FAT:	PROTEIN:	SODIUM:	CARBOHYDRATES:	SUGAR:	FIBER:
41	0.6 gram	1.1 grams	24 milligrams	9.4 grams	5.3 grams	1.5 grams

Strawberry Meringue Smoothie

Save your extra yolks from this recipe and add them to a simple egg scramble or frittata. To your egg dish, add mushrooms, onions, tomatoes, bacon . . . or whatever your taste buds crave. Serve it up with this heavenly smoothie for a powerhouse meal of nutrition, taste, and happy friends and family.

Recipe Yields: 3–4 cups

2 cups mixed greens
3 pastured egg whites
3 cups frozen strawberries, stems removed
1–2 teaspoons raw honey (depending on the
**   sweetness of the strawberries)**
2 cups unsweetened almond milk

1. Blend egg whites on high speed until frothy.
2. Add remaining ingredients and blend on high until smooth.
3. Add more liquid if necessary.

NUTRITIONAL INFORMATION (PER SERVING SIZE): (WITH 2 TEASPOONS OF HONEY)

CALORIES:	FAT:	PROTEIN:	SODIUM:	CARBOHYDRATES:	SUGAR:	FIBER:
77	1.3 grams	3.9 grams	139 milligrams	14.0 grams	8.2 grams	2.6 grams

Chocolate-Hazelnut Smoothie

Living a Paleo lifestyle doesn't include putting that addictive chocolate-hazelnut spread (you know the one) on toast in the mornings, so this smoothie is just for you. It is indulgent. It is rich. But it is also tasty and full of nutrition. Warning, this is a treat. Enter at your own risk and enjoy sparingly!

Recipe Yields: 3–4 cups

2 cups dandelion greens
3 small pears of choice, peeled and cored
⅛ cup hazelnuts
1 tablespoon unsweetened cocoa powder
2 tablespoons raw honey
2 cups unsweetened almond milk

1. Combine all ingredients and blend on high until smooth.
2. Add more liquid if necessary.

NUTRITIONAL INFORMATION (PER SERVING SIZE):

CALORIES:	FAT:	PROTEIN:	SODIUM:	CARBOHYDRATES:	SUGAR:	FIBER:
133	4.0 grams	2.5 grams	102 milligrams	25.2 grams	15.5 grams	5.3 grams

Coconut Nut Brownie Smoothie

With a name like this, how in the world can this smoothie be healthy? Well, unlike a traditional brownie loaded with flour, refined sugar, and dairy, this treat is overflowing with fiber, healthy fats, vitamin E, minerals, and antioxidants. But don't let the nutritional words fool you: This decadent dessert green smoothie is just plain delicious.

Recipe Yields: 3–4 cups

2 cups spring greens
1 small apple of choice, peeled and cored
½ avocado, peeled and pitted
½ cup unsweetened coconut flakes
2 tablespoons unsweetened cocoa powder
2 tablespoons raw honey
10 pecan halves
1½ cups coconut milk
8 coconut water ice cubes

1. Combine all ingredients and blend on high until smooth.
2. Add more liquid if necessary.

NUTRITIONAL INFORMATION (PER SERVING SIZE):

CALORIES:	FAT:	PROTEIN:	SODIUM:	CARBOHYDRATES:	SUGAR:	FIBER:
309	27.5 grams	3.9 grams	36 milligrams	15.4 grams	6.6 grams	4.3 grams

Raspberry-Lemon Tart Smoothie

Iceberg lettuce gets a bad rap, but surprisingly, it has a great natural carbohydrate count, which aids in the functioning of the nervous system. It also contains vitamins K and A, so don't count this leafy green out when making this timeless and delicious combination of raspberries and lemons.

Recipe Yields: 3–4 cups

1½ cups iceberg lettuce
4 mint leaves
2 cups frozen raspberries
½ peeled and frozen banana
1 lemon, peeled and seeded
1 cup lemon tea, cooled
1 cup unsweetened almond milk
1 tablespoon raw honey, optional

1. Combine all ingredients and blend on high until smooth.
2. Add more liquid if necessary.

NUTRITIONAL INFORMATION (PER SERVING SIZE): (WITHOUT HONEY)

CALORIES:	FAT:	PROTEIN:	SODIUM:	CARBOHYDRATES:	SUGAR:	FIBER:
65	0.7 gram	1.7 grams	43 milligrams	13.9 grams	5.8 grams	5.7 grams

Figgy Pudding Smoothie

Stop singing about it and just drink it! Charles Dickens would be proud. Take the refined sugar and bleached flour out of the traditional recipe and kick back by the fireplace with this nutrition-filled smoothie of figs, dates, and nut milk. One sip of this and your non-Paleo pals will make it part of their tradition too.

Recipe Yields: 3–4 cups

2 cups spinach
4 figs
1 peeled and frozen banana
1 tablespoon unsweetened cocoa powder
1 teaspoon orange zest
2 Medjool dates, pitted and minced
2 cups unsweetened almond milk

1. Combine all ingredients and blend on high until smooth.
2. Add more liquid if necessary.

NUTRITIONAL INFORMATION (PER SERVING SIZE):

CALORIES:	FAT:	PROTEIN:	SODIUM:	CARBOHYDRATES:	SUGAR:	FIBER:
117	1.7 grams	2.1 grams	92 milligrams	26.7 grams	19.8 grams	3.9 grams

Chocolate-Covered Cherry Smoothie

When cherry season hits, take advantage of these dark-red stone fruit beauties. Not only are they jam-packed with incredible flavonoids to protect your body against free radicals; their intense flavor and creaminess mask the bitterness that spinach and other greens may bring to your smoothie.

Recipe Yields: 3–4 cups

2 cups spinach
2 cups frozen pitted sweet cherries
1 banana
1 tablespoon unsweetened cocoa powder
1 tablespoon sunflower seeds
2 cups unsweetened almond milk

1. Combine all ingredients and blend on high until smooth.
2. Add more liquid if necessary.

NUTRITIONAL INFORMATION (PER SERVING SIZE):

CALORIES:	FAT:	PROTEIN:	SODIUM:	CARBOHYDRATES:	SUGAR:	FIBER:
95	2.9 grams	2.6 grams	93 milligrams	17.0 grams	10.7 grams	3.1 grams

CHAPTER 8
Weight Loss Smoothies

Paleo green smoothies are a great way to get a satisfying meal substitute when you're trying to shed a few pounds. They help suppress your appetite by providing a nutrient- and fiber-dense drink. If you are active while trying to lose weight, add a little protein to your smoothie by means of coconut oil, nuts, or almond butter. Or, have some hard-boiled eggs prepped and ready to eat with your smoothie. Being prepared is probably the number one thing you can do when losing weight. Unfortunately, we live in a world that offers food items that are quick, convenient . . . and unhealthy. Take a couple of hours at the beginning of each week to boil eggs, bake chicken, chop veggies, identify recipes to make, and freeze fruit for your smoothies. This will help set up your week for success.

Berry Pretty Smoothie

Blueberries, blackberries, strawberries, and raspberries are superfoods disguised as sweet treats. These fat-burning fruits are low in calories, packed with antioxidants that promote weight loss, and supply quick energy that allows you to burn fat fast. They are also rich in magnesium, one of the most important minerals in promoting energy regulation.

Recipe Yields: 3–4 cups

2 cups spinach
2 small apples of choice, peeled and cored
1 cup frozen mixed berries
½ lemon, peeled and seeded
1 cup water
1 cup unsweetened almond milk

1. Combine all ingredients and blend on high until smooth.
2. Add more liquid if necessary.

NUTRITIONAL INFORMATION (PER SERVING SIZE):

CALORIES:	FAT:	PROTEIN:	SODIUM:	CARBOHYDRATES:	SUGAR:	FIBER:
59	0.8 gram	1.2 grams	54 milligrams	13.3 grams	8.9 grams	2.6 grams

Metabolic Lemon Smoothie

Don't mistake that cute bright yellow lemon simply as a garnish. Lemons protect the immune system, boost your metabolism, and assist with weight loss. Throw away those sports drinks; lemons contain electrolytes such as potassium, magnesium, and calcium to help replenish the body after a heart-pumping workout.

Recipe Yields: 3–4 cups

**2 cups mixed greens
2 lemons, peeled and seeded
1 teaspoon lemon zest
1 cucumber, peeled
1 medium carrot, peeled
½" knob ginger, peeled
2 cups green tea, cooled**

1. Combine all ingredients and blend on high until smooth.
2. Add more liquid if necessary.

NUTRITIONAL INFORMATION (PER SERVING SIZE):

CALORIES:	FAT:	PROTEIN:	SODIUM:	CARBOHYDRATES:	SUGAR:	FIBER:
24	0.1 gram	1.1 grams	29 milligrams	6.6 grams	2.4 grams	2.0 grams

Dew Shrink My Waist Smoothie

Honeydew melon is a treat in the hot summer months. It also has a unique sweetness that helps curb your sweet tooth while protecting the body against free radicals, which cause inflammation in your body's cells. Smell your honeydew to make sure it is ripe. There should be a nice melon aroma. If not, let it sit on the counter for a couple days until it reaches peak.

Recipe Yields: 3–4 cups

1½ cups baby kale
6 mint leaves
½ cup frozen honeydew melon cubes
½ cup frozen peach cubes
½ small apple of choice, peeled and cored
1 cucumber, peeled
Juice and zest of ½ lime
2 cups water

1. Combine all ingredients and blend on high until smooth.
2. Add more liquid if necessary.

NUTRITIONAL INFORMATION (PER SERVING SIZE):

CALORIES:	FAT:	PROTEIN:	SODIUM:	CARBOHYDRATES:	SUGAR:	FIBER:
43	0.1 gram	1.1 grams	11 milligrams	10.8 grams	7.9 grams	1.6 grams

Carrot-Apple-Kiwi Smoothie

Although what you put in your body is 80 percent of the equation for weight loss, exercise is essential as well. The addition of kiwi and almond butter makes this a great post-workout drink. Kiwis contain enzymes that aid absorption of the protein found in the almond butter. This smoothie delivers a tasty little present to your tired muscles.

Recipe Yields: 3–4 cups

2 cups spinach
4 mint leaves
2 small carrots, peeled
2 small apples of choice, peeled and seeded
2 kiwis, peeled
1 teaspoon almond butter
2 cups water

1. Combine all ingredients and blend on high until smooth.
2. Add more liquid if necessary.

NUTRITIONAL INFORMATION (PER SERVING SIZE):

CALORIES:	FAT:	PROTEIN:	SODIUM:	CARBOHYDRATES:	SUGAR:	FIBER:
74	0.9 gram	1.5 grams	34 milligrams	16.8 grams	11.1 grams	3.1 grams

Zucchini Zapper Smoothie

Zucchinis take on the flavor of the things around them. Inexpensive, low in calories, and filling, zucchinis are often used in weight reduction and diabetic programs. Interestingly enough, this green squash boasts more potassium than a banana.

Recipe Yields: 3–4 cups

2 cups rainbow chard
4 mint leaves
1 medium zucchini, peeled
1 orange, peeled and seeded
1 small tart apple, peeled and cored
2 cups green tea, cooled

1. Combine all ingredients and blend on high until smooth.
2. Add more liquid if necessary.

NUTRITIONAL INFORMATION (PER SERVING SIZE):

CALORIES:	FAT:	PROTEIN:	SODIUM:	CARBOHYDRATES:	SUGAR:	FIBER:
44	0.2 gram	1.3 grams	43 milligrams	10.8 grams	8.0 grams	2.1 grams

Sexy Mango Smoothie

Exotic, beautiful, and sweet . . . I want to be a mango! In addition to containing a variety of vitamins and healthy enzymes, these little sexy superfoods are also known to be aphrodisiacs due to their high level of vitamin E, which helps regulate sex hormones and boost sex drive. Bring sexy back with this smoothie.

Recipe Yields: 3–4 cups

2 cups baby spinach
1 cup fresh mango slices, peeled and pitted
1 small tart apple, peeled and cored
1 tablespoon pumpkin seeds
2 cups mint tea, cooled

1. Combine all ingredients and blend on high until smooth.
2. Add more liquid if necessary.

NUTRITIONAL INFORMATION (PER SERVING SIZE):

CALORIES:	FAT:	PROTEIN:	SODIUM:	CARBOHYDRATES:	SUGAR:	FIBER:
54	1.0 gram	1.4 grams	12 milligrams	11.2 grams	9.1 grams	1.5 grams

Rainbow of Success Smoothie

The pot of gold at the end of this rainbow is the incredible cup of nutrition this gorgeous, colorful array of fruits and vegetables yields. Your body will be dancing a jig while fighting off free radicals, boosting your metabolism, cleansing your colon, making your skin and hair shiny, and warding off cancer. Cheers to that, my friend!

Recipe Yields: 3–4 cups

1 cup arugula
1 beet plus top greens, peeled and diced
1 medium carrot plus top greens, peeled
½ peeled and frozen banana
¼ cup frozen blackberries
½ lemon, peeled and seeded
¼ teaspoon ground cinnamon
2 cups water

1. Combine all ingredients and blend on high until smooth.
2. Add more liquid if necessary.

NUTRITIONAL INFORMATION (PER SERVING SIZE):

CALORIES:	FAT:	PROTEIN:	SODIUM:	CARBOHYDRATES:	SUGAR:	FIBER:
38	0.2 gram	1.0 gram	37 milligrams	9.3 grams	5.2 grams	2.3 grams

Green Light Smoothie

You have the green light to go forward with this ultimate Paleo green smoothie. I dare you to drink this and not smile for the rest of the day, knowing that you just gave your body the ingredients to function properly, hydrate cells, support the liver, and improve digestion . . . just to name a few.

Recipe Yields: 3–4 cups

1 cup mixed greens
½ cup parsley leaves
1 cucumber, peeled
1 celery stalk, with leaves
1 small tart apple, peeled and cored
Juice and zest of a lime
1 kiwi, peeled
2 cups green tea, cooled

1. Combine all ingredients and blend on high until smooth.
2. Add more liquid if necessary.

NUTRITIONAL INFORMATION (PER SERVING SIZE):

CALORIES:	FAT:	PROTEIN:	SODIUM:	CARBOHYDRATES:	SUGAR:	FIBER:
41	0.1 gram	1.2 grams	22 milligrams	10.3 grams	6.2 grams	2.0 grams

Slim Shady Smoothie

This smoothie is a nutritional powerhouse for most people, but for some, the nightshades can be a nightmare. If you're struggling with autoimmune disease or are just sensitive to nightshades, they can cause inflammation and pain in joints as well as digestive discomfort. Nightshades include tomatoes, bell peppers, eggplant, and even paprika, just to name a few. You can find a complete list of them and some discussion of their role in the Paleo lifestyle here: *www.thepaleomom.com/2013/08/what-are-nightshades.html.*

Recipe Yields: 3–4 cups

2 cups spinach
2 large tomatoes
½ yellow bell pepper, seeded
2 small carrots, peeled
⅛ teaspoon smoked paprika
1½ cups water

1. Combine all ingredients and blend on high until smooth.
2. Add more liquid if necessary.

NUTRITIONAL INFORMATION (PER SERVING SIZE):

CALORIES:	FAT:	PROTEIN:	SODIUM:	CARBOHYDRATES:	SUGAR:	FIBER:
36	0.2 gram	1.7 grams	37 milligrams	8.0 grams	3.7 grams	2.4 grams

Beet the Bloat Smoothie

Beets lend a natural sweetness to this smoothie and aid in the detoxification process, especially if left uncooked. When heated, beets can lose some important nutrients such as betalains, which aid in the elimination of toxins from your body. Just a side note: Beets can cause your urine to turn red, so don't be alarmed!

Recipe Yields: 3–4 cups

1 cup watercress
2 small beets plus top greens, peeled and chopped
1 small carrot, peeled
½" knob ginger, peeled
1 tablespoon raw sunflower seeds
2 cups water

1. Combine all ingredients and blend on high until smooth.
2. Add more liquid if necessary.

NUTRITIONAL INFORMATION (PER SERVING SIZE):

CALORIES:	FAT:	PROTEIN:	SODIUM:	CARBOHYDRATES:	SUGAR:	FIBER:
38	1.0 gram	1.4 grams	53 milligrams	5.9 grams	3.5 grams	1.9 grams

Goji Go-Go Smoothie

Considered both a berry and an herb, goji berries have been receiving a lot of press, because many celebrities swear by them. But don't let the faddish nature of that sway you; Chinese medicine has been using goji berries for centuries. They also have a low glycemic index, which, when consumed, helps stave off cravings for starchy and sugary foods.

Recipe Yields: 3–4 cups

1 cup baby spinach
1 banana
1 cup frozen mixed berries
¼ cup goji berries
1" knob ginger, peeled
2 cups water

1. Combine all ingredients and blend on high until smooth.
2. Add more liquid if necessary.

NUTRITIONAL INFORMATION (PER SERVING SIZE):

CALORIES:	FAT:	PROTEIN:	SODIUM:	CARBOHYDRATES:	SUGAR:	FIBER:
66	0.1 gram	1.8 grams	29 milligrams	16.8 grams	6.6 grams	5.2 grams

Peachy Lychee Smoothie

Lychees can be found in Asian markets but are also starting to show up in mainstream grocery stores. Getting into a lychee is quite easy. Cut off the top end and then peel off the outer layer by pushing on the meat of the fruit. Then cut out the inner seed. Lychees can be enjoyed plain as a tropical snack, in salads, or in green smoothies.

Recipe Yields: 3–4 cups

2 cups mixed greens
6 mint leaves
1 cup frozen peach chunks
1 cup lychees (10–12), peeled and pitted
½ lime, peeled and seeded
1 tablespoon sunflower seeds
2 cups green tea, cooled

1. Combine all ingredients and blend on high until smooth.
2. Add more liquid if necessary.

NUTRITIONAL INFORMATION (PER SERVING SIZE):

CALORIES:	FAT:	PROTEIN:	SODIUM:	CARBOHYDRATES:	SUGAR:	FIBER:
75	1.2 grams	1.5 grams	17 milligrams	14.6 grams	10.8 grams	1.7 grams

Frisée Peach Smoothie

Green tea is packed with fat-burning catechin antioxidants that aid in weight loss. Using green tea instead of water in smoothies amplifies the fat-burning properties of the vitamin- and mineral-rich greens and produce. Make sure to steep the tea for the suggested amount of time to maximize antioxidant release and taste.

Recipe Yields: 3–4 cups

2 cups frisée
1 cup frozen peach chunks
2 small carrots, peeled
½ lime, peeled and seeded
2 cups green tea, cooled

1. Combine all ingredients and blend on high until smooth.
2. Add more liquid if necessary.

NUTRITIONAL INFORMATION (PER SERVING SIZE):

CALORIES:	FAT:	PROTEIN:	SODIUM:	CARBOHYDRATES:	SUGAR:	FIBER:
47	0.9 gram	0.9 gram	23 milligrams	8.7 grams	4.7 grams	2.0 grams

CHAPTER 9
Smoothies for Athletes and Recovery

Exercise is a crucial component of the Paleo lifestyle. For some people, Paleo equals CrossFit. For others, Paleo is simply an eating style. On his website, Robb Wolf, biochemist and bestselling author of *The Paleo Solution: The Original Human Diet*, has a post written by registered dietitian Amy Kubal called "Seven Shades of Paleo." It takes you from the lifestyle called "Militant Paleo" all the way to "WTF Paleo." Although the article speaks toward eating choices, these labels also apply to exercise. Here's the deal. Move. Just move. Whether you are flipping tires or dancing your mad salsa steps. Whether you are doing long runs on the weekends or sprinting between light jogging, find what makes exercise fun for you. You're likely to continue on a path of exercise throughout your life. After you figure out what you like, come home and make a beautiful Paleo green smoothie to refresh those worn-out muscles!

Cherry Barre Smoothie

Barre is an exercise that incorporates ballet, pilates, and yoga. The goal is to lengthen and strengthen the muscles through isometric movements without the impact and injuries that result from some forms of exercise. Barre is also a great stress reliever and helps you find balance with your body. Cherries play a role in sleep and cell regeneration due to the melatonin present in these little gems.

Recipe Yields: 3–4 cups

2 cups Swiss or rainbow chard
1 cup pitted sweet cherries
1 cup frozen seedless grapes
2 limes, peeled and seeded
2 tablespoons raw sunflower seeds
2 cups green tea, cooled
Handful of ice cubes as needed

1. Combine all ingredients and blend on high until smooth.
2. Add more liquid if necessary.

NUTRITIONAL INFORMATION (PER SERVING SIZE):

CALORIES:	FAT:	PROTEIN:	SODIUM:	CARBOHYDRATES:	SUGAR:	FIBER:
100	2.0 grams	2.0 grams	40 milligrams	18.4 grams	11.7 grams	2.8 grams

Tire-Flippin' Fantastic Smoothie

After a tough hour of flipping tires, pistols, and wall balls, your body will crave some nourishment and protein to help repair those muscles. This smoothie not only contains vitamins and flavor; the pumpkin seeds and almond butter offer protein. The creamy banana helps this smoothie go down smoothly and hit the spot.

Recipe Yields: 3–4 cups

2 cups kale
2 peeled and frozen bananas
1 tablespoon unsweetened cocoa powder
2 tablespoons pumpkin seeds
1 tablespoon almond butter
2 cups peppermint tea, cooled

1. Combine all ingredients and blend on high until smooth.
2. Add more liquid if necessary.

NUTRITIONAL INFORMATION (PER SERVING SIZE):

CALORIES:	FAT:	PROTEIN:	SODIUM:	CARBOHYDRATES:	SUGAR:	FIBER:
115	4.0 grams	3.2 grams	4 milligrams	16.3 grams	7.6 grams	3.0 grams

Popeye Arms Smoothie

Well, here's an interesting fact. Erich von Wolf, a German chemist, accidently gave a false report regarding spinach. He stated that it had 35 milligrams of iron per serving instead 3.5 milligrams (pesky little decimal point). According to one story, Paramount Pictures saw this and ran with it, making spinach Popeye's main staple. (According to another, less interesting, story, Popeye's creator chose spinach because of its vitamin A content.)

Recipe Yields: 3–4 cups

2 cups spinach
1 large pasteurized, pastured egg
2 cups frozen blueberries
2 teaspoons almond butter
1 teaspoon coconut oil
2 cups coconut water
1 tablespoon raw honey, optional

1. Combine all ingredients and blend on high until smooth.
2. Add more liquid if necessary.

NUTRITIONAL INFORMATION (PER SERVING SIZE): (WITHOUT HONEY)

CALORIES:	FAT:	PROTEIN:	SODIUM:	CARBOHYDRATES:	SUGAR:	FIBER:
95	3.7 grams	3.1 grams	61 milligrams	15.9 grams	11.5 grams	2.7 grams

After WOD Smoothie

Cindy, Diane, Amanda . . . and more! Why does everyone who finishes a CrossFit WOD (workout of the day) come out cursing these nice ladies' names? The WODs are named after females. Coach Glassman, founder and president of CrossFit, states, "I want to explain the workout once and then give it a name. I thought that anything that left you flat on your back, looking up at the sky asking, 'what just happened to me?' deserved a female's name." The benefits of the powerhouse list of ingredients in this smoothie are endless, but it mainly helps to counter the inflammatory elements due to daily stressors, and the protein from the eggs helps rebuild muscle.

Recipe Yields: 3–4 cups

2 cups spinach
2 pastured eggs from farm-raised hens
2 small apples of choice, cored and seeded
½ avocado, peeled and seeded
¼ teaspoon cinnamon
⅛ cup cashews
2 cups coconut milk
6–8 coconut water ice cubes

1. Combine all ingredients and blend on high until smooth.
2. Add more liquid if necessary.

NUTRITIONAL INFORMATION (PER SERVING SIZE):

CALORIES:	FAT:	PROTEIN:	SODIUM:	CARBOHYDRATES:	SUGAR:	FIBER:
352	28.9 grams	6.9 grams	75 milligrams	17.5 grams	8.8 grams	2.7 grams

Burpee Buster Smoothie

Oh, the burpee, the lovely little burpee. If you don't know what it is, then you've never done one. You should look it up, though. There are many variations on the standard four-count exercise and also many ways to do it wrong. Ask a coach or personal trainer to show you the correct form before you incorporate this tricky little guy into your routine. Finish your day with this smoothie to curb your sweet tooth and satisfy the needs of your body's cellular regeneration.

Recipe Yields: 3–4 cups

2 cups spring greens
½ avocado, peeled and pitted
1 cup frozen mixed berries
2 plums, peeled and pitted
2 teaspoons almond butter
2 cups coconut milk

1. Combine all ingredients and blend on high until smooth.
2. Add more liquid if necessary.

NUTRITIONAL INFORMATION (PER SERVING SIZE):

CALORIES:	FAT:	PROTEIN:	SODIUM:	CARBOHYDRATES:	SUGAR:	FIBER:
301	26.7 grams	3.9 grams	21 milligrams	13.3 grams	5.5 grams	3.5 grams

Running Man Smoothie

This thirst quencher can be enjoyed before or after a run. You want to constantly hydrate when exercising, including beforehand. This smoothie is a much better alternative to commercial sports drinks. You get some carbs from the spinach, sodium from the pinch of salt, and electrolytes from the pure coconut water. Mint and watermelon lend brightness of flavor to this smoothie.

Recipe Yields: 3–4 cups

2 cups spinach
6 mint leaves
2 cups frozen, seeded watermelon chunks
6 pecan halves
Pinch of salt
2 cups coconut water

1. Combine all ingredients and blend on high until smooth.
2. Add more liquid if necessary.

NUTRITIONAL INFORMATION (PER SERVING SIZE):

CALORIES:	FAT:	PROTEIN:	SODIUM:	CARBOHYDRATES:	SUGAR:	FIBER:
64	1.7 grams	1.4 grams	68 milligrams	11.9 grams	9.7 grams	0.9 gram

Yoga Zen Smoothie

Find your inner yogi with this zentastic green smoothie. Ginger is a powerful anti-inflammatory food, which aids in digestion and helps to relieve nausea. And, quite honestly, it just tastes good. Remember, a little bit goes a long way, but if you want extra spice, throw in some more ginger for a little zip.

Recipe Yields: 3–4 cups

2 cups chopped romaine lettuce
2 small pears of choice, cored and peeled
1 cucumber, peeled
1" knob ginger, peeled
2 cups chamomile tea, cooled
1 tablespoon hemp seeds
1 tablespoon raw honey, optional

1. Combine all ingredients and blend on high until smooth.
2. Add more liquid if necessary.

NUTRITIONAL INFORMATION (PER SERVING SIZE): (WITHOUT HONEY)

CALORIES:	FAT:	PROTEIN:	SODIUM:	CARBOHYDRATES:	SUGAR:	FIBER:
77	1.3 grams	1.9 grams	4 milligrams	14.1 grams	8.5 grams	3.4 grams

Swimmer's Dream Smoothie

Whether you're doing the crawl or the backstroke, close your eyes and imagine this post-work-out tropical smoothie that is sure to have you dreaming of the beach. Frozen pineapple and banana replace ice cubes. Not only will this ensure your drink is not watered down, but the icy consistency of the smoothie is divine!

Recipe Yields: 3–4 cups

2 cups spring greens
½ cup frozen pineapple
½ lime, peeled and seeded
1 orange, peeled and seeded
½ peeled and frozen banana
⅛ cup sunflower seeds
2 cups coconut water

1. Combine all ingredients and blend on high until smooth.
2. Add more liquid if necessary.

NUTRITIONAL INFORMATION (PER SERVING SIZE):

CALORIES:	FAT:	PROTEIN:	SODIUM:	CARBOHYDRATES:	SUGAR:	FIBER:
98	2.1 grams	1.9 grams	36 milligrams	18.0 grams	10.7 grams	2.5 grams

Lift Like a Girl(!) Smoothie

Move over, boys; the girls can kick butt too! Lifting is an essential part of building lean muscle mass. And the more mass you have, the faster your metabolism will work, even when you are resting. So, lift away and do your body good. And afterward, bottoms up on this smoothie, because among other ingredients and their benefits, the vitamin K from the Asian pear can assist in maintaining the regular functioning of your blood.

Recipe Yields: 3–4 cups

1 cup spinach
1 cup kale
2 Asian pears, peeled and seeded
½ cup goji berries
1 tablespoon sunflower seeds
1 teaspoon coconut oil
2 cups coconut water

1. Combine all ingredients and blend on high until smooth.
2. Add more liquid if necessary.

NUTRITIONAL INFORMATION (PER SERVING SIZE):

CALORIES:	FAT:	PROTEIN:	SODIUM:	CARBOHYDRATES:	SUGAR:	FIBER:
119	2.3 grams	3.4 grams	76 milligrams	24.8 grams	11.3 grams	8.7 grams

Leg Day Recovery Smoothie

Squat. Lunge. Deadlift. Repeat. Repeat again. Then morning comes along. It is impossible to get out of bed or even climb into your car. That means you did good. You worked your legs thoroughly. Now go enjoy your Paleo green smoothie and help those muscles repair. Enjoy this smoothie containing almond butter as a protein source for rebuilding your beautiful quads!

Recipe Yields: 3–4 cups

2 cups kale
2 cups frozen mixed berries
1 banana
1 teaspoon almond butter
1 large, pastured egg
2 cups coconut water

1. Combine all ingredients and blend on high until smooth.
2. Add more liquid if necessary.

NUTRITIONAL INFORMATION (PER SERVING SIZE):

CALORIES:	FAT:	PROTEIN:	SODIUM:	CARBOHYDRATES:	SUGAR:	FIBER:
89	1.8 grams	2.9 grams	52 milligrams	16.8 grams	10.6 grams	2.4 grams

3K Smoothie

The three Ks in this smoothie refer to the kale, blackberries, and cucumber, which all deliver a healthy dose of vitamin K. Vitamin K protects against cancer and heart disease and helps in blood clotting. If you want a colder smoothie, try using cooled green tea or coconut water ice cubes for flavorful additions.

Recipe Yields: 3–4 cups

2 cups kale
2 cups frozen blackberries
1 cucumber, peeled
2 teaspoons almond butter
2 cups water

1. Combine all ingredients and blend on high until smooth.
2. Add more liquid if necessary.

NUTRITIONAL INFORMATION (PER SERVING SIZE):

CALORIES:	FAT:	PROTEIN:	SODIUM:	CARBOHYDRATES:	SUGAR:	FIBER:
76	2.0 grams	2.2 grams	9 milligrams	14.5 grams	9.3 grams	4.8 grams

What the Hill Smoothie

Whether you are hitting the open road or killing a spin class, cycling can burn some serious calories. Adding coconut oil to a pre-workout smoothie can give you longer-lasting energy. Because it is a "good" fat and fat burns slower than carbohydrates, it is exactly what you need to help power through and get up and down those hills.

Recipe Yields: 3–4 cups

2 cups mixed greens
2 cups frozen strawberries
1 banana, peeled
¼ cup cashews
2 teaspoons coconut oil
1 cup unsweetened almond milk
1 cup water

1. Combine all ingredients and blend on high until smooth.
2. Add more liquid if necessary.

NUTRITIONAL INFORMATION (PER SERVING SIZE):

CALORIES:	FAT:	PROTEIN:	SODIUM:	CARBOHYDRATES:	SUGAR:	FIBER:
127	6.6 grams	2.4 grams	61 milligrams	17.1 grams	7.4 grams	2.8 grams

Dancing Diva Smoothie

Breaking a sweat doesn't always have to be intense or painful. Sometimes you just need to get with a group of friends and shake your groove thing, whether in a gym class or on the dance floor. Living with a healthy mindset leads to eating well, moving your body, and having a positive outlook on life. Cool down when you exit the dance floor with this electrolyte-full smoothie to balance out your hip-shakin' workout!

Recipe Yields: 3–4 cups

2 cups spinach
4 mandarins or tangerines, peeled and seeded
2 small pears of choice, peeled and cored
1 tablespoon toasted sesame seeds
2 cups coconut water

1. Combine all ingredients and blend on high until smooth.
2. Add more liquid if necessary.

NUTRITIONAL INFORMATION (PER SERVING SIZE):

CALORIES:	FAT:	PROTEIN:	SODIUM:	CARBOHYDRATES:	SUGAR:	FIBER:
127	2.1 grams	2.2 grams	45 milligrams	28.1 grams	20.1 grams	4.5 grams

The Replenisher Smoothie

I'd like to see a team pour a cooler of this over the head of a winning coach. This smoothie is full of electrolytes to help replenish your body after a workout. Containing vitamins, carbohydrates, sodium, fiber, and electrolytes, this soothing drink gives your muscles and tissues lots of TLC to help them do their jobs properly.

Recipe Yields: 3–4 cups

2 cups kale
1 cooked small sweet potato, cooled
1 cup cantaloupe
1 tablespoon almond butter
Pinch of sea salt
2 cups water
Handful of ice cubes, optional

1. Combine all ingredients and blend on high until smooth.
2. Add more liquid if necessary.

NUTRITIONAL INFORMATION (PER SERVING SIZE):

CALORIES:	FAT:	PROTEIN:	SODIUM:	CARBOHYDRATES:	SUGAR:	FIBER:
86	2.2 grams	2.5 grams	65 milligrams	15.0 grams	6.7 grams	2.7 grams

CHAPTER 10
Smoothies for Cleansing and Detox

Do you ever feel like your body just needs a break? Well, so do a lot of people in the Paleo community. They incorporate intermittent fasting into their diets, for numerous reasons. Skipping a meal or two lets your body rest from oxidative stress or free radicals induced from foods. It is helpful for losing weight, cancer patients, and athletes. But do your research before taking this on for any length of time. There are many ways to go about this. Some people fast between twenty-four and thirty-six hours. Some skip meals periodically. Some allow for "feeding windows," whereby they will fast and only eat one meal a day. Do whatever you are comfortable with and whatever works for your lifestyle. Our bodies have been accustomed to this type of eating since prehistoric days. Although the cavemen skipped meals out of necessity, our bodies are set up to function without food at certain times. This is why we have fat stores to accommodate for starvation periods. Drinking a Paleo green smoothie helps give your body a break from solid foods. In a sense, the blender does the digesting for you.

It is also crucial that you choose organic foods during this process as ingesting pesticides would counteract the progress you are trying to make during a cleansing and detoxification phase. So make your body happy and sub out a few meals or a few days with nutrient-rich smoothies.

Cleansing Cranberry Smoothie

If you are looking for a cooling and tangy treat or relief from a urinary tract infection (UTI), or both, this cleansing smoothie is for you. If you are prone to UTIs, this smoothie can be a protective measure that will make the urinary tract more acidic and make it less likely bacteria will hang around. Please remember that these smoothies are preventative measures, not cures.

Recipe Yields: 3–4 cups

2 cups watercress
2 cups cranberries
1 cucumber, peeled
½ medium lemon, peeled and seeded
½" knob ginger, peeled
2 cups water

1. Combine all ingredients and blend on high until smooth.
2. Add more liquid if necessary.

NUTRITIONAL INFORMATION (PER SERVING SIZE):

CALORIES:	FAT:	PROTEIN:	SODIUM:	CARBOHYDRATES:	SUGAR:	FIBER:
35	0.1 gram	1.0 gram	13 milligrams	8.8 grams	3.1 grams	3.2 grams

Broccoli for Bladder Health Smoothie

Broccoli probably isn't the superfood that comes to mind when you think of cleansing, but this cruciferous veggie provides far more vitamins and nutrients than you would think. A single serving of broccoli includes the important vitamins A, B, C, and K along with fiber, zinc, folate, magnesium, iron, and beta-carotene.

Recipe Yields: 3–4 cups

1 cup arugula
1 cup chopped broccoli
3 small apples of choice, peeled and cored
½ medium lemon, peeled and seeded
1 teaspoon coconut oil
2 cups water

1. Combine all ingredients and blend on high until smooth.
2. Add more liquid if necessary.

NUTRITIONAL INFORMATION (PER SERVING SIZE):

CALORIES:	FAT:	PROTEIN:	SODIUM:	CARBOHYDRATES:	SUGAR:	FIBER:
70	1.4 grams	1.2 grams	13 milligrams	15.6 grams	10.8 grams	2.4 grams

Carrot Cleanser Smoothie

Harnessing the powerful vitamins and minerals contained in carrots while you're on a detox cleanse can help in many ways. The beta-carotene that gives carrots their vibrant color is not only important for eye health; it also protects cells against free radicals and promotes optimal cell functioning.

Recipe Yields: 3–4 cups

2 cups spinach
5 small carrots, peeled
2 limes, peeled and seeded
2 cups green tea, cooled

1. Combine all ingredients and blend on high until smooth.
2. Add more liquid if necessary.

NUTRITIONAL INFORMATION (PER SERVING SIZE):

CALORIES:	FAT:	PROTEIN:	SODIUM:	CARBOHYDRATES:	SUGAR:	FIBER:
39	0.2 gram	1.2 grams	56 milligrams	10.3 grams	3.6 grams	3.0 grams

Fiber Flush Smoothie

With the fiber of the greens, apples, and cauliflower and the soothing effect of the ginger, this recipe makes for the perfect combination for optimizing digestion. You can alleviate stomach discomfort with this tasty combo. Ginger is also an anti-gas aid as it relaxes tension in the gastrointestinal tract. Introduce ginger tea to your nighttime routine and you should be ready to go by morning.

Recipe Yields: 3–4 cups

1½ cups kale
¼ cup chopped cauliflower
2 small apples of choice, peeled and cored
½ lime, peeled and seeded
½" knob ginger, peeled
2 cups ginger tea, cooled

1. Combine all ingredients and blend on high until smooth.
2. Add more liquid if necessary.

NUTRITIONAL INFORMATION (PER SERVING SIZE):

CALORIES:	FAT:	PROTEIN:	SODIUM:	CARBOHYDRATES:	SUGAR:	FIBER:
39	0.2 gram	0.6 gram	4 milligrams	10.6 grams	7.1 grams	1.5 grams

Glad Gallbladder Smoothie

A cleansed and healthy gallbladder is one free of toxins and waste, and is able to function properly. If there's a problem with it, digestion can be a difficult and painful process. By promoting a healthy gallbladder, you are ensuring the digestive process moves as smoothly and regularly as possible.

Recipe Yields: 3–4 cups

2 cups spinach
1 cup chopped asparagus spears (hard, woody ends discarded)
½ lemon, peeled and seeded
1 small apple of choice, peeled and cored
1 Roma tomato
1 garlic clove
2 cups water

1. Combine all ingredients and blend on high until smooth.
2. Add more liquid if necessary.

NUTRITIONAL INFORMATION (PER SERVING SIZE):

CALORIES:	FAT:	PROTEIN:	SODIUM:	CARBOHYDRATES:	SUGAR:	FIBER:
37	0.4 gram	1.6 grams	18 milligrams	8.7 grams	5.7 grams	1.9 grams

Liven Up Your Liver Smoothie

The liver is an important organ responsible for removing toxins from your body. It is the best cleanser of your body, so treat it well. Beets, beet greens, and apples are known to optimize liver functioning. The banana's smooth texture makes this a nutritional, tasty, liver-purifying blend.

Recipe Yields: 3–4 cups

2 cups beet greens
1 beet, peeled and chopped
1 small tart apple, peeled and cored
1 peeled and frozen banana
2 cups water

1. Combine all ingredients and blend on high until smooth.
2. Add more liquid if necessary.

NUTRITIONAL INFORMATION (PER SERVING SIZE):

CALORIES:	FAT:	PROTEIN:	SODIUM:	CARBOHYDRATES:	SUGAR:	FIBER:
54	0.1 gram	1.2 grams	63 milligrams	13.7 grams	8.4 grams	2.5 grams

Green Garlic Smoothie

This pungent, unique smoothie will not only cleanse your senses but your digestive system as well. Garlic is the little powerhouse bulb that makes a big impact. Loaded with sulphur, garlic helps cleanse by producing enzymes that aid in filtering toxins and ridding the digestive tract of bacteria.

Recipe Yields: 3–4 cups

2 cups arugula
1 celery stalk, with leaves
1 zucchini
3–4 garlic cloves
2 cups green tea, cooled

1. Combine all ingredients and blend on high until smooth.
2. Add more liquid if necessary.

NUTRITIONAL INFORMATION (PER SERVING SIZE):

CALORIES:	FAT:	PROTEIN:	SODIUM:	CARBOHYDRATES:	SUGAR:	FIBER:
17	0.2 gram	1.1 grams	16 milligrams	3.4 grams	1.6 grams	0.9 gram

Colorful Cleansing Smoothie

It may be difficult to figure out which food group is best for your body. The answer is . . . all of them! The easiest route to achieving optimum health is to taste the rainbow. Eat a variety of different foods with a rainbow of vibrant colors to ensure your body is receiving abundant vitamins and nutrients. This smoothie is a step on that colorful road.

Recipe Yields: 3–4 cups

2 cups mixed greens
1 beet with greens, peeled and chopped
2 parsnips, peeled
2 oranges, peeled and seeded
2 cups black tea, cooled

1. Combine all ingredients and blend on high until smooth.
2. Add more liquid if necessary.

NUTRITIONAL INFORMATION (PER SERVING SIZE):

CALORIES:	FAT:	PROTEIN:	SODIUM:	CARBOHYDRATES:	SUGAR:	FIBER:
98	0.3 gram	2.2 grams	45 milligrams	24.6 grams	11.7 grams	5.5 grams

Strawberry-Rhubarb Healing Smoothie

Strawberry and rhubarb, anyone? Yes, please! Rhubarb contains antioxidants, including lyco-pene and anthocyanins, which have been known to help fight cancer. It also contains a healthy amount of vitamin K, which helps your blood clot when needed and protects your bones. But one of the great benefits of rhubarb is its powerful astringency and ability to aid in cleansing and detoxification.

Recipe Yields: 3–4 cups

2 cups spinach
2 stalks rhubarb
1 cup frozen strawberries, stems removed
2 cups green tea, cooled
2 tablespoons raw honey, optional

1. Combine all ingredients and blend on high until smooth.
2. Add more liquid if necessary.

NUTRITIONAL INFORMATION (PER SERVING SIZE): (WITHOUT HONEY)

CALORIES:	FAT:	PROTEIN:	SODIUM:	CARBOHYDRATES:	SUGAR:	FIBER:
22	0.1 gram	0.8 gram	14 milligrams	5.4 grams	2.0 grams	1.6 grams

Ginger Apple Smoothie

Ginger is hailed as one of nature's most potent medicinal plants; it's best known for relieving stomach ailments. Combining ginger with the fiber found in fruits and leafy greens is an effective way to clean out the digestive tract, promote the release of good digestive enzymes, and soothe the stomach.

Recipe Yields: 3–4 cups

1 cup turnip greens
1 cup spinach
2 small tart apples, peeled and cored
1 small turnip, peeled
1" knob ginger, peeled
2 cups white tea, cooled

1. Combine all ingredients and blend on high until smooth.
2. Add more liquid if necessary.

NUTRITIONAL INFORMATION (PER SERVING SIZE):

CALORIES:	FAT:	PROTEIN:	SODIUM:	CARBOHYDRATES:	SUGAR:	FIBER:
41	0.1 gram	0.8 gram	21 milligrams	10.8 grams	7.4 grams	1.8 grams

Alcohol Recovery Smoothie

Because alcohol can really do a number on your liver, it is important to supply your body with the best foods possible to maintain this organ's optimal functioning following heavy alcohol consumption. Spinach, carrots, apples, beets, lemon, and grapefruit have shown to be true superfoods when it comes to purging the liver of harmful toxins. In addition, these foods are high in vitamin C and promote health, while minimizing feelings of moodiness and depression.

Recipe Yields: 3–4 cups

2 cups spinach
1 small carrot, peeled
1 small beet, peeled
1 small tart apple, peeled and cored
½ lemon, peeled and seeded
½ grapefruit, peeled and seeded
2 cups green tea, cooled

1. Combine all ingredients and blend on high until smooth.
2. Add more liquid if necessary.

NUTRITIONAL INFORMATION (PER SERVING SIZE):

CALORIES:	FAT:	PROTEIN:	SODIUM:	CARBOHYDRATES:	SUGAR:	FIBER:
47	0.1 gram	1.2 grams	37 milligrams	11.8 grams	5.6 grams	1.9 grams

Green Clean Smoothie

This smoothie is an easy one to remember. Just grab anything green! This drink gives true meaning to the phrase "Paleo green smoothie" and is loaded with vitamins and minerals. As with all the recipes in this book, use this as a guide and tailor it to your taste buds and needs. If you don't have celery on hand, throw in some asparagus . . . it is all good for you and there are no wrong choices.

Recipe Yields: 3–4 cups

2 cups spinach
2 celery stalks, including leaves
2 small tart apples, peeled and cored
2 kiwis, peeled
2 cups water

1. Combine all ingredients and blend on high until smooth.
2. Add more liquid if necessary.

NUTRITIONAL INFORMATION (PER SERVING SIZE):

CALORIES:	FAT:	PROTEIN:	SODIUM:	CARBOHYDRATES:	SUGAR:	FIBER:
58	0.4 gram	1.1 grams	33 milligrams	14.6 grams	10.1 grams	2.5 grams

CHAPTER 11
Smoothies for Health and Disease Prevention

Fresh, organic produce is good for your body for many reasons related to the healing vitamins and minerals that are introduced to your system without the added chemicals and pesticides that non-organic produce contains. Diversity is also important—change your habits and consume the rainbow of fruits and vegetables available to you. Each piece of produce has its own makeup of vitamins and minerals that help different organs and body functions do what they were meant to do. Drinking Paleo green smoothies allows you to combine a variety of these healthy ingredients in a quick, portable meal. Avocados lend creaminess to smoothies as well as being a great preventative ingredient in the fight against oral cancer. Roasting carrots before blending adds a natural sweetness while giving your body a dose of beta-carotene, converted into vitamin A to support a healthy immune system and good eye health. So, drink up for good taste and to prevent health problems.

The Pollinator Smoothie

Suffering from asthma or allergies? Pick up some bee pollen from a local farmers' market or beekeeper. Bee pollen is a wild powder collected by bees from plants and flowers. Granules from this powder are formed as they are accumulated on the bee until it takes it back to the hive and starts all over. Local pollen is preferable because it is collected from the very things in your area that may be aggravating your allergies. Ingesting the pollen works under the same premise as receiving an immunization. It slowly introduces your body to the irritant so that it can build up antibodies to ward off a future infection or irritation.

Recipe Yields: 3–4 cups

2 cups mixed greens
3 medium pears of choice, peeled and cored
1 tablespoon local bee pollen
2 teaspoons raw honey (local is best)
2 cups green tea, cooled

1. Combine all ingredients and blend on high until smooth.
2. Add more liquid if necessary.

NUTRITIONAL INFORMATION (PER SERVING SIZE):

CALORIES:	FAT:	PROTEIN:	SODIUM:	CARBOHYDRATES:	SUGAR:	FIBER:
91	0.5 gram	1.6 grams	19 milligrams	22.5 grams	14.5 grams	4.6 grams

Mango Digestion Smoothie

Mangos aid digestion by combating acidity and uncomfortable acids in the digestive system; they create a more placid, balanced system and promote a smooth, regular digestive process. The apple and the arugula in this smoothie are high in fiber and the coconut water is full of electrolytes, which will keep your body hydrated and prevent constipation.

Recipe Yields: 3–4 cups

2 cups arugula
1½ cups frozen mango cubes
1 small apple of choice, peeled and cored
½" knob ginger, peeled
2 cups coconut water

1. Combine all ingredients and blend on high until smooth.
2. Add more liquid if necessary.

NUTRITIONAL INFORMATION (PER SERVING SIZE):

CALORIES:	FAT:	PROTEIN:	SODIUM:	CARBOHYDRATES:	SUGAR:	FIBER:
85	0.1 gram	0.6 gram	34 milligrams	21.8 grams	18.8 grams	1.6 grams

Cocoa Strong Smoothie

Almost every commercial candy bar available consists of milk products, refined sugar, and manufactured fillers, so the Paleo community is left to create desserts at home. Purchase unsweetened cocoa or 80 percent dark chocolate bars, and you can turn your kitchen into a chocolate shop of homemade delectable delights. By consuming strong cancer-fighting antioxidants, you can extend your life while satisfying your chocolate addiction.

Recipe Yields: 3–4 cups

2 cups spinach
1 cup frozen mixed berries
1 banana
4 pecan halves
1 tablespoon unsweetened cocoa powder
2 cups unsweetened almond milk

1. Combine all ingredients and blend on high until smooth.
2. Add more liquid if necessary.

NUTRITIONAL INFORMATION (PER SERVING SIZE):

CALORIES:	FAT:	PROTEIN:	SODIUM:	CARBOHYDRATES:	SUGAR:	FIBER:
72	2.6 grams	1.9 grams	92 milligrams	12.0 grams	5.7 grams	3.0 grams

Breathe Easy Smoothie

Rich, plump blackberries are not just a tasty treat; they are also packed with a variety of vitamins and minerals that can aid in overall health. Specifically, the magnesium content in blackberries helps relax the muscles and thin the mucus most commonly associated with breathing difficulties.

Recipe Yields: 3–4 cups

2 cups spinach
1 cup frozen blackberries
1 cup frozen pitted cherries
8 almonds
2 cups unsweetened almond milk

1. Combine all ingredients and blend on high until smooth.
2. Add more liquid if necessary.

NUTRITIONAL INFORMATION (PER SERVING SIZE):

CALORIES:	FAT:	PROTEIN:	SODIUM:	CARBOHYDRATES:	SUGAR	FIBER:
74	2.7 grams	2.2 grams	92 milligrams	11.2 grams	7.7 grams	3.1 grams

Dude Food Smoothie

Men are from Mars . . . well, you know the story. Not only do the genders think differently; our bodies are set up differently. The smoothie below is geared toward men. The tomatoes and watermelon contain lycopene, which protects against prostate cancer. The hazelnuts and kale help boost testosterone levels. And don't skip the sunflower seeds. They improve your sex drive!

Recipe Yields: 3–4 cups

2 cups kale
2 Roma tomatoes
1 cup frozen watermelon cubes
8 hazelnuts
1 tablespoon sunflower seeds
2 cups water

1. Combine all ingredients and blend on high until smooth.
2. Add more liquid if necessary.

NUTRITIONAL INFORMATION (PER SERVING SIZE):

CALORIES:	FAT:	PROTEIN:	SODIUM:	CARBOHYDRATES:	SUGAR:	FIBER:
76	4.5 grams	2.2 grams	10 milligrams	8.4 grams	5.8 grams	1.6 grams

Cantaloupe for Cancer Prevention Smoothie

One of the major responsibilities of the strong antioxidant beta-carotene is to combat free radicals we get from environmental toxins, certain foods, and unhealthy lifestyles. Free radicals can cause abnormal growth in cells, which can lead to dangerous illnesses including cancer. Studies have shown that diets rich in carotenes promote healthy cell growth, thereby reducing the chance of cancers and other diseases.

Recipe Yields: 3–4 cups

2 cups watercress
2 cups frozen cantaloupe cubes
1 banana
1 tablespoon sunflower seeds
2 cups water

1. Combine all ingredients and blend on high until smooth.
2. Add more liquid if necessary.

NUTRITIONAL INFORMATION (PER SERVING SIZE):

CALORIES:	FAT:	PROTEIN:	SODIUM:	CARBOHYDRATES:	SUGAR:	FIBER:
66	1.1 grams	1.8 grams	23 milligrams	13.8 grams	9.8 grams	1.8 grams

Deep Sleep Smoothie

A good night's sleep is sometimes an overlooked step in a healthy lifestyle. But not only is sound slumber good for beauty and eliminating those under-eye circles, it can improve memory, slow down inflammation, and help you live longer. One of the benefits people talk about when first adopting a Paleo lifestyle is the incredible sleep they get. This is due largely to a change in diet and consumption of fresh, organic foods.

Recipe Yields: 3–4 cups

2 cups spinach
2 cups pitted cherries
1 peeled and frozen banana
½ teaspoon ground nutmeg
2 cups unsweetened almond milk
1 tablespoon raw honey, optional

1. Combine all ingredients and blend on high until smooth.
2. Add more liquid if necessary.

NUTRITIONAL INFORMATION (PER SERVING SIZE): (WITHOUT HONEY)

CALORIES:	FAT:	PROTEIN:	SODIUM:	CARBOHYDRATES:	SUGAR:	FIBER:
94	1.5 grams	2.1 grams	92 milligrams	19.8 grams	13.6 grams	2.8 grams

The Kitchen Sink Smoothie

Diseases have individual origins and causes, but the dangers posed by free radicals and oxidative processes and their contribution to debilitating illnesses are well known. The antioxidants in fruits and vegetables combat these types of sickness. By including berries, greens, and a colorful assortment of fruits and veggies in your diet, you're increasing your chances of living a longer, healthier life.

Recipe Yields: 3–4 cups

2 cups mixed greens
1 small tart apple, peeled and cored
½ peeled and frozen banana
1 celery stalk, including leaves
1 small parsnip, peeled and cubed
½ orange, peeled and seeded
½ teaspoon vanilla extract or seeds from ½ vanilla bean
2 cups unsweetened almond milk
Handful of ice cubes, optional

1. Combine all ingredients and blend on high until smooth.
2. Add more liquid if necessary.

NUTRITIONAL INFORMATION (PER SERVING SIZE):

CALORIES:	FAT:	PROTEIN:	SODIUM:	CARBOHYDRATES:	SUGAR:	FIBER:
96	1.4 grams	1.9 grams	108 milligrams	20.9 grams	10.7 grams	3.5 grams

Amazing Avocado Smoothie

Although avocados have been found to fight the free radicals in colon, breast, and prostate cancer, the most notable protective benefit they create in the human body is protection against oral cancer. With a 50 percent mortality rate, most commonly due to late detection, oral cancer is preventable. You can help fight against it with the addition of just two ounces of avocado per day to your diet.

Recipe Yields: 3–4 cups

1½ cups spinach
½ cup cilantro
2 avocados, peeled and pitted
3 small carrots, peeled
1 lime, peeled and seeded
4 walnut halves
2 cups water

1. Combine all ingredients and blend on high until smooth.
2. Add more liquid if necessary.

NUTRITIONAL INFORMATION (PER SERVING SIZE):

CALORIES:	FAT:	PROTEIN:	SODIUM:	CARBOHYDRATES:	SUGAR:	FIBER:
160	13.0 grams	2.6 grams	46 milligrams	12.6 grams	2.4 grams	7.1 grams

Roasted Carrot Smoothie

By roasting carrots in the oven at 350°F for 30 minutes, you bring out their sweetness by caramelizing the natural sugars. Try this technique with peppers, garlic, parsnips, and whatever else you'd like to experiment with. The unique flavors that roasting brings out can completely change the taste profile of your green smoothie.

Recipe Yields: 3–4 cups

2 cups mixed greens
3 roasted carrots, cooled
1 small apple of choice, peeled and cored
½ orange, peeled and seeded
1 tablespoon pumpkin seeds
2 cups water

1. Combine all ingredients and blend on high until smooth.
2. Add more liquid if necessary.

NUTRITIONAL INFORMATION (PER SERVING SIZE):

CALORIES:	FAT:	PROTEIN:	SODIUM:	CARBOHYDRATES:	SUGAR:	FIBER:
59	2.2 grams	1.4 grams	46 milligrams	10.9 grams	6.8 grams	2.3 grams

Celery for Diabetic Health Smoothie

The sodium content in celery plays an important role in a diabetic's diet. When you consume this delicious vegetable, your body is more efficient in regulating and maintaining water balance. This crisp veggie is rich in vitamins A, C, K, B6, and B1, as well as calcium, potassium, fiber, and folate, and is also a natural diuretic.

Recipe Yields: 3–4 cups

2 cups arugula
2 celery stalks, with leaves
½ bell pepper (color of choice), seeded
1 Roma tomato
3–4 garlic cloves
2 cups water

1. Combine all ingredients and blend on high until smooth.
2. Add more liquid if necessary.

NUTRITIONAL INFORMATION (PER SERVING SIZE):

CALORIES:	FAT:	PROTEIN:	SODIUM:	CARBOHYDRATES:	SUGAR:	FIBER:
23	0.3 gram	1.0 gram	25 milligrams	4.6 grams	2.6 grams	1.1 grams

Energetic Artichoke Smoothie

Although artichokes are most commonly used in salads and appetizers, raw artichokes make for a tasty addition to Paleo green smoothies such as this one and are high in carbohydrates, making them an instant source of energy. Artichokes pack a protective punch against colon cancer, inflammation, and bone loss.

Recipe Yields: 3–4 cups

2 cups spinach
4 artichoke hearts
1 small tart apple, peeled and cored
1 medium carrot, peeled
2 cups green tea, cooled

1. Combine all ingredients and blend on high until smooth.
2. Add more liquid if necessary.

NUTRITIONAL INFORMATION (PER SERVING SIZE):

CALORIES:	FAT:	PROTEIN:	SODIUM:	CARBOHYDRATES:	SUGAR:	FIBER:
50	0.1 gram	2.6 grams	91 milligrams	12.2 grams	5.0 grams	6.1 grams

Turnip Turnaround Smoothie

One of the many reasons raw-food enthusiasts adopt and adhere to their lifestyle is the drop in vitamins, minerals, and nutrients when produce is heated above a certain temperature. Blending veggies raw in a Paleo green smoothie is a delicious way to enjoy these superfoods, protect against a number of cancers, and promote eye health.

Recipe Yields: 3–4 cups

1 cup green leaf lettuce
1 turnip including top greens, peeled
2 small carrots, peeled
2 small pears of choice, peeled and seeded
2 cups white tea, cooled

1. Combine all ingredients and blend on high until smooth.
2. Add more liquid if necessary.

NUTRITIONAL INFORMATION (PER SERVING SIZE):

CALORIES:	FAT:	PROTEIN:	SODIUM:	CARBOHYDRATES:	SUGAR:	FIBER:
52	0.2 gram	0.7 gram	24 milligrams	13.7 grams	8.5 grams	3.1 grams

CHAPTER 12
Anti-Aging and Radiant Skin Smoothies

One of the main reasons to follow a Paleo diet is because it concentrates on real food. The processed foods that line the aisles of the grocery store are aging us. The artificial inflammatory ingredients they contain are destroying our bodies, inside and out. They can cause a host of ailments and diseases such as heart disease, joint pain, cancers, diabetes, and much more. Paleo green smoothies give us a step up by providing a variety of nutrients and phytochemicals in one meal, aiding in cell function and repair. Although you can't stop getting older, your biological health is measured by how resilient your cells are. How much vitality you have as you progress into old age is determined by healthy cell growth; this shows outwardly by your shiny eyes, white teeth, and clear and hydrated skin. By eating a variety of greens, fruits, vegetables, and herbs, the inflammation is reduced in your body. So, drink up . . . it's your fountain of youth!

Tropical Youth Smoothie

Luscious fruits such as kiwi, pineapple, and strawberries blend perfectly with delicious vitamin- and mineral-rich romaine. When making green smoothies, it is natural to throw everything into your blender. However, fruits can be different. Strawberry stems emit a poison to ward off pesky critters and protect the black strawberry seeds. Although not lethal to humans, ingesting the stems can be a source of gut discomfort.

Recipe Yields: 3–4 cups

2 cups romaine lettuce
4 mint leaves
1 kiwi, peeled
1 cup frozen and cubed pineapple
1 cup frozen strawberries, stems removed
4 walnut halves
2 cups spearmint tea, cooled

1. Combine all ingredients and blend on high until smooth.
2. Add more liquid if necessary.

NUTRITIONAL INFORMATION (PER SERVING SIZE):

CALORIES:	FAT:	PROTEIN:	SODIUM:	CARBOHYDRATES:	SUGAR:	FIBER:
64	1.5 grams	1.4 grams	2 milligrams	13.1 grams	4.6 grams	2.7 grams

Bone Health Smoothie

The magnesium in blackberries can do amazing things for respiratory relief and can also help create stronger bones. Because magnesium plays an important role in the absorption of calcium, a diet rich in this powerful mineral ensures healthy bones.

Recipe Yields: 3–4 cups

2 cups iceberg lettuce
4 mint leaves
1 cup frozen blackberries
½ cup frozen pineapple cubes
1 banana
2 cups unsweetened almond milk

1. Combine all ingredients and blend on high until smooth.
2. Add more liquid if necessary.

NUTRITIONAL INFORMATION (PER SERVING SIZE):

CALORIES:	FAT:	PROTEIN:	SODIUM:	CARBOHYDRATES:	SUGAR:	FIBER:
81	1.5 grams	1.7 grams	83 milligrams	16.6 grams	8.7 grams	3.4 grams

Peek-a-Boo Pomegranate Smoothie

The peek of pomegranate in this powerhouse drink packed with superfoods adds vitamins C and K, and folate. Pomegranates are also known to reverse damage done to our bodies by free radicals, thus slowing the aging process. Commercial pomegranate juice generally contains additives and filler ingredients such as cane sugar and corn syrup. In addition, the juice can be a little pricey. So, just make your own. Place your pomegranate seeds in a fine mesh strainer or sieve, and smoosh them with the back of a spoon. Catch the juice in a bowl. Voilà!

Recipe Yields: 3–4 cups

2 cups spinach
1 cup frozen raspberries
½ peeled and frozen banana
2 oranges, peeled and seeded
4 walnut halves
¼ cup pomegranate juice
1½ cups green tea, cooled

1. Combine all ingredients and blend on high until smooth.
2. Add more liquid if necessary.

NUTRITIONAL INFORMATION (PER SERVING SIZE):

CALORIES:	FAT:	PROTEIN:	SODIUM:	CARBOHYDRATES:	SUGAR:	FIBER:
89	1.5 grams	1.9 grams	14 milligrams	18.7 grams	11.9 grams	4.8 grams

Mental Makeover Smoothie

Hate forgetting things? Feel like you are absentminded a little too often? This smoothie is designed to get your brain back on track with rich sources of vitamins and minerals that stimulate and rejuvenate brain functions. In addition to being a rich source of iron and folate (which aids in iron absorption), this amazing smoothie holds a wealth of vitamins A, B, C, D, and K that provide cancer-fighting power against liver, ovarian, colon, and prostate cancers.

Recipe Yields: 3–4 cups

2 cups spinach
2 cucumbers, peeled
2 celery stalks plus leaves
1 large tomato
2 cups black tea, cooled
3 ice cubes
Pinch of sea salt, optional
Freshly grated horseradish, optional garnish

1. Combine all ingredients except horseradish and blend on high until smooth.
2. Add more liquid if necessary.
3. Garnish with fresh horseradish if desired.

NUTRITIONAL INFORMATION (PER SERVING SIZE): (WITHOUT ADDED SALT)

CALORIES:	FAT:	PROTEIN:	SODIUM:	CARBOHYDRATES:	SUGAR:	FIBER:
24	0.1 gram	1.4 grams	31 milligrams	4.9 grams	2.5 grams	1.7 grams

Gravity Schmavity Smoothie

There are superfoods . . . and then there are berries. Rich in color and taste, these little babies pack a punch with flavonoids, polyphenols, probiotics, antioxidants, and vitamins. Berries help protect against free radicals, which can help against dry and sagging skin due to gravity and life. Although premature aging and cell degeneration can't be stopped, you can curtail the signs with healthy foods. Add berries to your daily routine for pretty skin, shiny hair, and a healthy heart.

Recipe Yields: 3–4 cups

2 cups spinach
2 cups frozen mixed berries
⅛ cup hazelnuts
1 tablespoon raw honey
2 cups green tea, cooled

1. Combine all ingredients and blend on high until smooth.
2. Add more liquid if necessary.

NUTRITIONAL INFORMATION (PER SERVING SIZE):

CALORIES:	FAT:	PROTEIN:	SODIUM:	CARBOHYDRATES:	SUGAR:	FIBER:
62	2.6 grams	1.3 grams	12 milligrams	9.6 grams	6.5 grams	2.0 grams

An Apple a Day Smoothie

Not only does an apple a day keep the doctor away, but it may also keep the wrinkles away. Loaded with quercetin, a potent antioxidant, apples can aid in the fight against free radicals. In addition, the glutathione found in spinach fights against aging and dementia. Drink this smoothie for the beautiful side effects, but enjoy it for the taste.

Recipe Yields: 3–4 cups

2 cups spinach
2 small apples of choice, peeled and cored
2 small carrots, peeled
1 teaspoon ground cinnamon
¼ teaspoon ground nutmeg
¼ teaspoon vanilla extract or seeds from ¼ vanilla bean
2 cups unsweetened almond milk

1. Combine all ingredients and blend on high until smooth.
2. Add more liquid if necessary.

NUTRITIONAL INFORMATION (PER SERVING SIZE):

CALORIES:	FAT:	PROTEIN:	SODIUM:	CARBOHYDRATES:	SUGAR:	FIBER:
62	1.4 grams	1.4 grams	109 milligrams	12.0 grams	8.0 grams	2.3 grams

Cocoa-Raspberry Brainiac Smoothie

Chocolate and raspberries are an incredibly delicious combination . . . but use whatever berries you have on hand for this brainy smoothie. There is strong evidence that berries help counter age-related memory loss and dementia, and promote overall brain health. Berries are easy to freeze and can be enjoyed year-round for health and wellness.

Recipe Yields: 3–4 cups

2 cups butter lettuce
2 cups frozen raspberries
¼ cup frozen seedless grapes
1 tablespoon unsweetened cocoa powder
4 walnut halves
2 cups unsweetened almond milk

1. Combine all ingredients and blend on high until smooth.
2. Add more liquid if necessary.

NUTRITIONAL INFORMATION (PER SERVING SIZE):

CALORIES:	FAT:	PROTEIN:	SODIUM:	CARBOHYDRATES:	SUGAR:	FIBER:
77	2.8 grams	2.4 grams	82 milligrams	11.7 grams	4.9 grams	5.6 grams

Glowing Beauty Smoothie

Containing both pumpkin and carrot, this creamy indulgence is full of carotenes. The human body converts carotene into vitamin A, which is necessary for cell growth and skin support. If you have a little pumpkin purée left over after making this smoothie, whisk an egg into it and give yourself a facial. The pumpkin will protect you from age spots, the yolk is full of nourishment, and the egg white tightens skin.

Recipe Yields: 3–4 cups

2 cups green leaf lettuce
½ cup pumpkin purée
1 medium carrot, peeled
½ avocado, peeled and pitted
¼ teaspoon ground cinnamon
¼ teaspoon vanilla extract or seeds from ¼ vanilla bean
1 tablespoon pumpkin seeds
2 cups green tea, cooled

1. Combine all ingredients and blend on high until smooth.
2. Add more liquid if necessary.

NUTRITIONAL INFORMATION (PER SERVING SIZE):

CALORIES:	FAT:	PROTEIN:	SODIUM:	CARBOHYDRATES:	SUGAR:	FIBER:
57	3.5 grams	1.6 grams	18 milligrams	5.4 grams	1.5 grams	2.8 grams

Toothy Grin Smoothie

This smoothie's variety of powerful antioxidants will make you look and feel younger. The vitamin C in the oranges is fantastic for healthy gums, the fiber in apples works as a natural tooth cleaner, and the apple cider vinegar is excellent for whiter teeth and eliminating bad breath.

Recipe Yields: 3–4 cups

2 cups spring greens
6 mint leaves
1 medium apple of choice, peeled and cored
2 oranges, peeled and seeded
1 kiwi, peeled
1 teaspoon apple cider vinegar (or more if you can handle it)
2 cups water

1. Combine all ingredients and blend on high until smooth.
2. Add more liquid if necessary.

NUTRITIONAL INFORMATION (PER SERVING SIZE):

CALORIES:	FAT:	PROTEIN:	SODIUM:	CARBOHYDRATES:	SUGAR:	FIBER:
65	0.2 gram	1.1 grams	5 milligrams	16.5 grams	12.2 grams	3.0 grams

Pineapple Express Smoothie

Set a piece of pineapple aside before making this smoothie and rub it all over your face to help unclog your pores. The alpha hydroxyl acids will help clear up your face. Afterward, drink this delicious smoothie to help keep your skin hydrated and supple. The result is a younger looking face.

Recipe Yields: 3–4 cups

2 cups spinach
1½ cups pineapple chunks
½ cup frozen strawberries, stems removed
2 cups unsweetened almond milk

1. Combine all ingredients and blend on high until smooth.
2. Add more liquid if necessary.

NUTRITIONAL INFORMATION (PER SERVING SIZE):

CALORIES:	FAT:	PROTEIN:	SODIUM:	CARBOHYDRATES:	SUGAR:	FIBER:
55	1.3 grams	1.3 grams	92 milligrams	10.4 grams	7.0 grams	1.6 grams

Spa Skin Smoothie

Fruits are essential for beautiful, supple skin. They provide many nutrients that fight destructive free radicals and reduce inflammation. Inflammation not only causes internal diseases, but contributes to signs of aging on the exterior also. Drinking this fruit-based smoothie can help slow the process of impending wrinkles, dry and sagging skin, and fine lines.

Recipe Yields: 3–4 cups

2 cups spring greens
½ cup frozen strawberries, stems removed
1 cup frozen mango cubes
1 medium carrot, peeled
1 orange, peeled and seeded
6 walnut halves
2 cups coconut water

1. Combine all ingredients and blend on high until smooth.
2. Add more liquid if necessary.

NUTRITIONAL INFORMATION (PER SERVING SIZE):

CALORIES:	FAT:	PROTEIN:	SODIUM:	CARBOHYDRATES:	SUGAR:	FIBER:
103	2.1 grams	1.5 grams	47 milligrams	21.4 grams	16.8 grams	2.8 grams

Peaches 'n Cream Complexion Smoothie

Loaded with vitamins A and C, peaches are a wonderful fruit to add to your internal regime for a beautiful glowing complexion and skin that's elastic and supple. Here's a little natural treat for your skin: Rub the peaches directly on your skin. Peaches contain alpha hydroxyl acids that help remove dark spots and eye circles, as well as minimizing and tightening pores.

Recipe Yields: 3–4 cups

2 cups mixed greens
6 ripe peaches, peeled and pitted
1 tablespoon sunflower seeds
2 cups unsweetened almond milk

1. Combine all ingredients and blend on high until smooth.
2. Add more liquid if necessary.

NUTRITIONAL INFORMATION (PER SERVING SIZE):

CALORIES:	FAT:	PROTEIN:	SODIUM:	CARBOHYDRATES:	SUGAR:	FIBER:
120	2.5 grams	3.2 grams	96 milligrams	21.3 grams	18.9 grams	2.4 grams

Honey Citrus Smoothie

After making this antioxidant-rich green smoothie, save those citrus peels. They make excellent additions to homemade facial scrubs. Let them dry out and then pulse them in your food processor or coffee grinder. Add the ground rind to a little plain Greek yogurt and some honey and there you have it: a facial mask free of chemicals that works wonders and costs pennies.

Recipe Yields: 3–4 cups

2 cups spring greens
3 oranges, peeled and seeded
1 medium lemon, peeled and seeded
1 lime, peeled and seeded
2 tablespoons raw honey
1–2 cups water

1. Combine all ingredients and blend on high until smooth.
2. Add more liquid if necessary.

NUTRITIONAL INFORMATION (PER SERVING SIZE):

CALORIES:	FAT:	PROTEIN:	SODIUM:	CARBOHYDRATES:	SUGAR:	FIBER:
92	0.2 gram	1.3 grams	10 milligrams	24.4 grams	19.1 grams	3.7 grams

CHAPTER 13
Kid-Friendly Smoothies

Kid-friendly smoothies are a great way to be sneaky with fruits and veggies for your picky eaters (perfect for some spouses too . . . you know who you are!). By and large, Americans purchase oranges, apples, bananas, cucumbers, iceberg lettuce, and carrots on a regular basis. These items are familiar and are usually received positively by family members. But bring home some mustard greens, parsnips, fresh basil, and a coconut and you'll probably see some confused faces. Smoothies take away some of this apprehension by combining many flavors and nutrients to make this newness less scary. Get your little cavekids involved. Ask them to pick out an unfamiliar fruit or vegetable each week and let them assist in choosing a recipe. Whether you get a good or bad flavor result each week, adventures in the kitchen create lasting memories for you and your family. Be a little silly and have fun in the kitchen.

Dinosaur Snot Smoothie

Who knew that dinosaur snot could be so healthy and tasty? Okay, okay, it's a gross name but it may be perfect for the playful cavekid who likes to be silly—and who may be a little skeptical about trying a green drink. Laughing is a great part of learning and why not have a little fun in the kitchen?

Recipe Yields: 3–4 cups

2 cups spinach
1 cup frozen blackberries
1 peeled and frozen banana
2 oranges, peeled and seeded
2 cups water

1. Combine all ingredients and blend on high until smooth.
2. Add more liquid if necessary.

NUTRITIONAL INFORMATION (PER SERVING SIZE):

CALORIES:	FAT:	PROTEIN:	SODIUM:	CARBOHYDRATES:	SUGAR:	FIBER:
85	0.3 gram	1.7 grams	16 milligrams	21.3 grams	14.1 grams	4.7 grams

Monkeying Around Smoothie

This one's perfect for the spinach haters in your house. The little monkeys will come running when you whip up this smoothie in the blender. The sweetness of the bananas and almond milk will help mask the spinach and parsnip, helping to make this drink a family favorite.

Recipe Yields: 3–4 cups

2 cups spinach
2 peeled and frozen bananas
1 tablespoon unsweetened cocoa powder
1 parsnip, peeled
2 cups unsweetened almond milk

1. Combine all ingredients and blend on high until smooth.
2. Add more liquid if necessary.

NUTRITIONAL INFORMATION (PER SERVING SIZE):

CALORIES:	FAT:	PROTEIN:	SODIUM:	CARBOHYDRATES:	SUGAR:	FIBER:
102	1.7 grams	2.4 grams	96 milligrams	21.6 grams	9.2 grams	3.8 grams

Green Lemonade Smoothie

You may not be setting up a green lemonade stand in front of your house anytime soon, but you can win the hearts of your little ones with this smoothie. The mango provides creaminess and sweetness that neutralizes a little of the tartness from the citrus acid in the lemons. If the mangos aren't super-ripe, you may want to add a little raw honey to taste.

Recipe Yields: 3–4 cups

2 cups mixed greens
3 small lemons, peeled and seeded
1 cup frozen mango cubes
Zest of 1 lemon
4 walnut halves
2 cups coconut water
1–2 teaspoons raw honey, optional

1. Combine all ingredients and blend on high until smooth.
2. Add more liquid if necessary.

NUTRITIONAL INFORMATION (PER SERVING SIZE): (WITHOUT HONEY)

CALORIES:	FAT:	PROTEIN:	SODIUM:	CARBOHYDRATES:	SUGAR:	FIBER:
78	1.5 grams	1.3 grams	48 milligrams	18.0 grams	12.9 grams	2.3 grams

X-Ray Vision Smoothie

After drinking this smoothie, you'll be able to see through the walls and spy on your brother or sister. Well, not really, but our bodies do convert the carotenes in the carrots and apricots to vitamin A, which is an important nutrient for overall eye health. So, drink up and *see* the healthy results.

Recipe Yields: 3–4 cups

2 cups leafy greens
2 medium carrots, peeled
2 apricots, peeled and seeded
½ cup frozen seedless grapes
¼ cup frozen mixed berries
1 tablespoon raw honey
2 cups water

1. Combine all ingredients and blend on high until smooth.
2. Add more liquid if necessary.

NUTRITIONAL INFORMATION (PER SERVING SIZE):

CALORIES:	FAT:	PROTEIN:	SODIUM:	CARBOHYDRATES:	SUGAR:	FIBER:
60	0.2 gram	1.0 gram	30 milligrams	15.2 grams	11.7 grams	2.1 grams

Tropic Twister Smoothie

Add this smoothie to your staycation plans to round out the experience. Another way to get kids to enjoy these green smoothies is to let them pick out a special "smoothie" cup at the store. The key is getting them involved. Or hollow out a pineapple and let them drink this one island-style . . . in a grass skirt, if that's what it takes.

Recipe Yields: 3–4 cups

2 cups iceberg lettuce
1 cup frozen pineapple cubes
1 kiwi, peeled
½ banana, peeled
1 cup mango cubes, peeled and pitted
2 cups coconut milk

1. Combine all ingredients and blend on high until smooth.
2. Add more liquid if necessary.

NUTRITIONAL INFORMATION (PER SERVING SIZE):

CALORIES:	FAT:	PROTEIN:	SODIUM:	CARBOHYDRATES:	SUGAR:	FIBER:
299	22.9 grams	3.6 grams	18 milligrams	22.3 grams	10.7 grams	2.7 grams

Green Snowball Fight Smoothie

Snowball fiiiight! Let the little ones sprinkle their own coconut garnish on top of their smoothies. You can ask them to make it snow on their drinks. Of course, this portion of the task is messy, so this is not for the neat freaks . . . unless teaching children the importance of cleaning up after themselves is on the to-do list. It's a two-for-one. Healthy and clean kids!

Recipe Yields: 3–4 cups

2 cups baby spinach
1 cup unsweetened coconut flakes, plus extra for garnish
2 cups frozen mango cubes
1 peeled and frozen banana
2 cups coconut milk

1. Combine all ingredients and blend on high until smooth.
2. Add more liquid if necessary.
3. Garnish top of drink with coconut flakes to look like snow.

NUTRITIONAL INFORMATION (PER SERVING SIZE): (WITHOUT GARNISH)

CALORIES:	FAT:	PROTEIN:	SODIUM:	CARBOHYDRATES:	SUGAR:	FIBER:
412	32.7 grams	4.0 grams	31 milligrams	30.5 grams	18.7 grams	4.4 grams

Bomdiggity Smoothie

Just saying the name of this smoothie puts a smile on your face, and that's half the fun. With the presence of the banana and pear, this drink is super creamy, and the strawberries top it off with sweetness. This smoothie has kid-friendly ingredients and may be one of the "starter" drinks to ease them into Paleo green smoothies.

Recipe Yields: 3–4 cups

2 cups mixed greens
1 medium pear of choice, peeled and cored
½ cup frozen strawberries, stems removed
2 bananas
1 tablespoon sunflower seeds
2 cups unsweetened almond milk

1. Combine all ingredients and blend on high until smooth.
2. Add more liquid if necessary.

NUTRITIONAL INFORMATION (PER SERVING SIZE):

CALORIES:	FAT:	PROTEIN:	SODIUM:	CARBOHYDRATES:	SUGAR:	FIBER:
110	2.4 grams	2.0 grams	97 milligrams	23.2 grams	12.5 grams	3.8 grams

Bug Bite Smoothie

Garnish this smoothie with some plump, sweet blackberries and call them bugs. Drink that smoothie down or the bugs will bite you! Okay, this may only work with children who are used to sarcasm and silliness. Please don't scare the neighbors' kids. In any event, get them involved in washing and mixing the ingredients, and use organic produce whenever possible.

Recipe Yields: 3–4 cups

2 cups green leaf lettuce
4 mint leaves
1 cup blackberries, plus some for garnish
2 medium apples of choice, peeled and cored
2 cups unsweetened almond milk
1–2 teaspoons raw honey, optional

1. Combine all ingredients and blend on high until smooth.
2. Add more liquid if necessary.

NUTRITIONAL INFORMATION (PER SERVING SIZE): (WITHOUT HONEY OR GARNISH)

CALORIES:	FAT:	PROTEIN:	SODIUM:	CARBOHYDRATES:	SUGAR:	FIBER:
71	1.4 grams	1.5 grams	85 milligrams	14.4 grams	10.0 grams	3.3 grams

Silly Sour Smoothie

This is a fun one to make together with your little sous chef. First blend everything but the kiwis, banana, and honey. Do a taste test and savor the sour. Then add the kiwi. Does it taste different? Add in that creamy, sweet banana. Is it a little less sour? More creamy? Okay, now round it out with that yummy unrefined honey. This smoothie can be a fun lesson in learning about the different properties of fruits and what they add to the drink.

Recipe Yields: 3–4 cups

2 cups green leaf lettuce
½ grapefruit, peeled and seeded
1 medium lemon, peeled and seeded
1 lime, peeled and seeded
2 kiwis, peeled
1 banana
2 cups unsweetened almond milk
1–2 teaspoons raw honey, optional

1. Combine all ingredients and blend on high until smooth.
2. Add more liquid if necessary.

NUTRITIONAL INFORMATION (PER SERVING SIZE): (WITHOUT HONEY)

CALORIES:	FAT:	PROTEIN:	SODIUM:	CARBOHYDRATES:	SUGAR:	FIBER:
85	1.5 grams	1.9 grams	87 milligrams	18.3 grams	7.5 grams	2.9 grams

Strawberrylicious Smoothie

Aaah . . . fresh air. After a day of pickin' strawberries at your local farm, there is nothing more refreshing than a glassful of your hard work. Strawberries are not only a summer rock star in the taste department; they are packed with folate, vitamin C, and phytonutrients that will help lower your risk of developing certain diseases such as diabetes and high blood pressure.

Recipe Yields: 3–4 cups

2 cups mixed greens
1 small pear of choice, peeled and cored
2 cups frozen strawberries, stems removed
2 cups unsweetened almond milk
1–2 teaspoons raw honey, optional

1. Combine all ingredients and blend on high until smooth.
2. Add more liquid if necessary.

NUTRITIONAL INFORMATION (PER SERVING SIZE): (WITHOUT HONEY)

CALORIES:	FAT:	PROTEIN:	SODIUM:	CARBOHYDRATES:	SUGAR:	FIBER:
62	1.4 grams	1.2 grams	97 milligrams	13.2 grams	7.0 grams	3.0 grams

Monster Mash Smoothie

What a great smoothie to make in front of a group of lil' monster partygoers. Add in the spaghetti squash (brains), grapes (eyeballs), banana (yellow monster poop), almonds (fingernails), raw honey (critter snot), and the almond milk (albino bug blood). This is a healthy and fun option to the commercially made, junk-filled juice boxes and sodas. And, you'll be the cool parent . . . so how is this wrong?

Recipe Yields: 3–4 cups

2 cups mixed greens
1 cup cooked and cooled spaghetti squash
½ cup frozen seedless grapes
2 bananas
10 blanched almonds (one for each finger)
2 teaspoons raw honey
2 cups unsweetened almond milk

1. Combine all ingredients and blend on high until smooth.
2. Add more liquid if necessary.

NUTRITIONAL INFORMATION (PER SERVING SIZE):

CALORIES:	FAT:	PROTEIN:	SODIUM:	CARBOHYDRATES:	SUGAR:	FIBER:
124	3.5 grams	2.7 grams	104 milligrams	23.8 grams	14.2 grams	2.9 grams

Princess Potion Smoothie

Not every princess has to end up with the prince living happily ever after. Sometimes the princess can grow up to be a nutritionist and learn about the properties of fresh foods and their healthful qualities. The beets in this special potion are full of phytonutrients.

Recipe Yields: 3–4 cups

1½ cups spinach
2 beets plus greens, peeled and chopped
½ cup frozen blueberries
2 cups coconut water
1–2 teaspoons raw honey, optional

1. Combine all ingredients and blend on high until smooth.
2. Add more liquid if necessary.

NUTRITIONAL INFORMATION (PER SERVING SIZE): (WITHOUT HONEY)

CALORIES:	FAT:	PROTEIN:	SODIUM:	CARBOHYDRATES:	SUGAR:	FIBER:
52	0.2 gram	1.4 grams	82 milligrams	12.1 grams	9.3 grams	2.1 grams

Cherry Pit Spittin' Smoothie

If you are ever near Traverse City, Michigan, during the National Cherry Festival, stop by because it is all about beautiful cherries and family fun with orchard tours, concerts, parades, and so much more. But if you can't make it to the festival, give tribute by hosting your very own cherry pit spittin' contest!

Recipe Yields: 3–4 cups

2 cups Boston or Bibb lettuce
1 cup frozen pitted sweet cherries
1 peeled and frozen banana
1 teaspoon vanilla extract or seeds from 1 vanilla bean
2 cups coconut milk

1. Combine all ingredients and blend on high until smooth.
2. Add more liquid if necessary.

NUTRITIONAL INFORMATION (PER SERVING SIZE):

CALORIES:	FAT:	PROTEIN:	SODIUM:	CARBOHYDRATES:	SUGAR:	FIBER:
273	22.3 grams	3.3 grams	16 milligrams	14.9 grams	7.5 grams	1.7 grams

Tater for Tots Smoothie

To encourage Southern farmers to grow sweet potatoes, botanist George Washington Carver came up with over 100 ways to use this tasty tuber. Besides just eating them baked or fried, or adding them to a smoothie, Mr. Carver found that you could make vinegar, molasses, and postage stamp glue from sweet potatoes—to name a few of his discoveries. Can you guess the other uses? Look it up and see how many you guessed.

Recipe Yields: 3–4 cups

2 cups arugula
1 medium cooked sweet potato, cooled
½ cup frozen blueberries
1 small tart apple, peeled and cored
1 teaspoon ground cinnamon
6 pecan halves
2 cups water

1. Combine all ingredients and blend on high until smooth.
2. Add more liquid if necessary.

NUTRITIONAL INFORMATION (PER SERVING SIZE):

CALORIES:	FAT:	PROTEIN:	SODIUM:	CARBOHYDRATES:	SUGAR:	FIBER:
70	1.7 grams	1.2 grams	17 milligrams	13.7 grams	7.1 grams	2.6 grams

Righteous Raspberry Cocoa Smoothie

We know a raspberry is a beautiful little berry—a superfood full of antioxidants. But do you know another definition of *raspberry*? Derived from British comedy, it is also a term for the noise you make when you press your lips together and blow. The added avocado will not only lend a healthy fat to this drink, but also an enjoyable creaminess.

Recipe Yields: 3–4 cups

2 cups Boston or Bibb lettuce
1 cup raspberries
1 avocado, peeled and pitted
1 teaspoon vanilla extract or seeds from 1 vanilla bean
2 tablespoons unsweetened cocoa
2 tablespoon pure maple syrup
2 cups almond milk

1. Combine all ingredients and blend on high until smooth.
2. Add more liquid if necessary.

NUTRITIONAL INFORMATION (PER SERVING SIZE):

CALORIES:	FAT:	PROTEIN:	SODIUM:	CARBOHYDRATES:	SUGAR:	FIBER:
153.2	9.4 grams	2.8 grams	100.7 milligrams	17.8 grams	8.1 grams	6.9 grams

Twinkle, Twinkle, Little Starfruit Smoothie

Starfruit, also known as carambola, contains folates and riboflavin while the waxy exterior has a good amount of fiber. The entire fruit is edible, including the skin. Before processing them into the smoothie, slice them into cross sections so your little ones can see the perfect star shapes. Maybe they can even make a wish before adding it to the mix!

Recipe Yields: 3–4 cups

2 cups spinach
2 starfruit
1 cup frozen mixed berries
Juice of ½ orange
2 cups lemon tea, cooled

1. Combine all ingredients and blend on high until smooth.
2. Add more liquid if necessary.

NUTRITIONAL INFORMATION (PER SERVING SIZE):

CALORIES:	FAT:	PROTEIN:	SODIUM:	CARBOHYDRATES:	SUGAR:	FIBER:
42.6	.22 grams	1.2 grams	16.8 milligrams	9.6 grams	5.9 grams	2.4 grams

CHAPTER 14
Smoothies for Pregnancy and Prenatal Care

There is nothing more magical than growing another little human being in your body. It is a beautiful gift with which we have been entrusted. Care for your baby starts before conception by preparing your body with nutrients such as folate, iron, and all of the other necessary vitamins and minerals your body craves to function properly. Living the Paleo lifestyle is perfect for this time in your life as whole foods and pesticide-free, organic produce are right at the center of this diet.

Of course, you'll likely encounter some challenges along the way. You may suffer from nausea, swollen ankles, moodiness, heartburn, and a whole slew of commonplace occurrences over the next several months . . . or you may sail right through (if you are in the latter category, don't share this fact with other pregnant women). Eat and drink what you can. Some weeks will seem repetitive because only a handful of foods may be appetizing to you. But there is light at the end of the tunnel and your bundle of joy will be driving you crazy soon enough! Here are several different types of smoothies to help you along your journey.

Nausea No More Smoothie

Anyone who has been pregnant is perplexed by the term "morning sickness," as we know that this disturbance can hit at any time of the day. Bananas are not only a creamy and soothing food that is easy on the stomach, but they contain potassium and B vitamins to keep your body nourished.

Recipe Yields: 3–4 cups

2 cups Bibb or Boston lettuce
2 peeled and frozen bananas
½ cup frozen blueberries
2 cups unsweetened almond milk

1. Combine all ingredients and blend on high until smooth.
2. Add more liquid if necessary.

NUTRITIONAL INFORMATION (PER SERVING SIZE):

CALORIES:	FAT:	PROTEIN:	SODIUM:	CARBOHYDRATES:	SUGAR:	FIBER:
80	1.5 grams	1.6 grams	81 milligrams	16.5 grams	9.1 grams	2.4 grams

Mango Maternity Smoothie

In addition to being velvety and soothing, this exotic smoothie is high in folate due to the spinach and mango. Folate is required in a woman's diet to help prevent birth defects. This is a great prenatal drink to add to your diet as folate is especially necessary before conception and during the first months of pregnancy.

Recipe Yields: 3–4 cups

2 cups spinach
2 cups frozen mango cubes
½ cup frozen pineapple cubes
2 cups coconut milk

1. Combine all ingredients and blend on high until smooth.
2. Add more liquid if necessary.

NUTRITIONAL INFORMATION (PER SERVING SIZE):

CALORIES:	FAT:	PROTEIN:	SODIUM:	CARBOHYDRATES:	SUGAR:	FIBER:
297	22.7 grams	2.9 grams	26 milligrams	22.7 grams	14.6 grams	2.0 grams

Cranbaby Smoothie

Women are susceptible to urinary tract infections (UTIs) during pregnancy. Cranberries can be very helpful as a preventative during this time as it is believed that the antioxidants present in them can prevent certain bacteria from sticking to the walls of the urinary tract and causing an infection.

Recipe Yields: 3–4 cups

2 cups kale
1 cup cranberries
1 cup frozen mixed berries
2 cups unsweetened almond milk
1–2 teaspoons pure maple syrup, optional

1. Combine all ingredients and blend on high until smooth.
2. Add more liquid if necessary.

NUTRITIONAL INFORMATION (PER SERVING SIZE): (WITHOUT MAPLE SYRUP)

CALORIES:	FAT:	PROTEIN:	SODIUM:	CARBOHYDRATES:	SUGAR:	FIBER:
45	1.4 grams	1.2 grams	83 milligrams	7.4 grams	3.2 grams	2.7 grams

Tummy Love Smoothie

Ginger has long been used for nausea and morning sickness. Just be careful: It can also cause heartburn in some mommies. A knob of ginger can be difficult to peel because of the grooves and bumps. Instead, use a spoon's edge to scrape away the skin. It's much easier than trying to use a vegetable peeler . . . your fingertips will thank you.

Recipe Yields: 3–4 cups

2 cups spinach
2 small apples of choice, peeled and cored
2 small carrots, peeled
½" knob ginger, peeled
¼ teaspoon ground cinnamon
2 cups unsweetened almond milk

1. Combine all ingredients and blend on high until smooth.
2. Add more liquid if necessary.

NUTRITIONAL INFORMATION (PER SERVING SIZE):

CALORIES:	FAT:	PROTEIN:	SODIUM:	CARBOHYDRATES:	SUGAR:	FIBER:
60	1.4 grams	1.4 grams	109 milligrams	11.5 grams	7.9 grams	2.0 grams

Cankles Be Gone Smoothie

Swollen ankles are common during pregnancy due to water retention. Give yourself a break from standing. While soaking your swollen feet in a warm Epsom salt bath (it is the miracle cure for sore muscles also), sip this smoothie full of potassium and antioxidants known for reducing swelling.

Recipe Yields: 3–4 cups

2 cups spinach
1 cup cantaloupe, peeled and seeded
1 orange, peeled and seeded
1 medium carrot, peeled
2 cups coconut water

1. Combine all ingredients and blend on high until smooth.
2. Add more liquid if necessary.

NUTRITIONAL INFORMATION (PER SERVING SIZE):

CALORIES:	FAT:	PROTEIN:	SODIUM:	CARBOHYDRATES:	SUGAR:	FIBER:
60	0.1 gram	1.4 grams	60 milligrams	14.5 grams	11.9 grams	2.0 grams

Bundle of C Smoothie

This refreshing smoothie is bursting with vitamin C. The natural powers in oranges, strawberries, and sweet peppers are necessary for the formation of collagen, which works naturally to help form the cartilage, tendons, bones, and skin of your growing bundle of joy.

Recipe Yields: 3–4 cups

2 cups spinach
1 orange, peeled and seeded
1 cup strawberries, stems removed
½ red bell pepper, seeded
2 cups coconut water

1. Combine all ingredients and blend on high until smooth.
2. Add more liquid if necessary.

NUTRITIONAL INFORMATION (PER SERVING SIZE):

CALORIES:	FAT:	PROTEIN:	SODIUM:	CARBOHYDRATES:	SUGAR:	FIBER:
57	0.2 gram	1.3 grams	44 milligrams	13.5 grams	10.5 grams	2.2 grams

Lil' Punkin Smoothie

Take care of your growing lil' punkin with this soothing blend of pumpkin and spices. When pregnant, your hips, back, and abdomen start to stretch and loosen in preparation for the birth. The protein in pumpkin seeds will help repair and prepare your muscles. Also, for a snack, drizzle the seeds with a little avocado oil and bake them until crispy. Let cool, and enjoy.

Recipe Yields: 3–4 cups

2 cups mixed greens
½ cup pumpkin purée
1 peeled and frozen banana
2 tablespoons pumpkin seeds
½ teaspoon pumpkin pie spice
2 cups unsweetened almond milk

1. Combine all ingredients and blend on high until smooth.
2. Add more liquid if necessary.

NUTRITIONAL INFORMATION (PER SERVING SIZE):

CALORIES:	FAT:	PROTEIN:	SODIUM:	CARBOHYDRATES:	SUGAR:	FIBER:
67	3.0 grams	2.4 grams	97 milligrams	9.3 grams	4.2 grams	1.9 grams

Berry Bump Smoothie

When mama's happy, everyone's happy! Satisfying and refreshing ingredients combine in this flavorful smoothie that's packed with a large number of minerals and vitamins required for prenatal support and development. Constipation is a common occurrence during pregnancy; the goji berries in this smoothie work as a natural laxative.

Recipe Yields: 3–4 cups

2 cups romaine lettuce
¼ cup goji berries
¼ cup frozen blueberries
1 kiwi, peeled
1 celery stalk
1 apple, cored and peeled
2 cups coconut water

1. Combine all ingredients and blend on high until smooth.
2. Add more liquid if necessary.

NUTRITIONAL INFORMATION (PER SERVING SIZE):

CALORIES:	FAT:	PROTEIN:	SODIUM:	CARBOHYDRATES:	SUGAR:	FIBER:
82	0.2 gram	2.0 grams	60 milligrams	20.2 grams	11.9 grams	4.9 grams

Hot Mama Smoothie

Spicy foods are perfectly safe to eat when you're pregnant. With that said, they're a personal preference because heartburn is a common ailment during pregnancy. Spicy foods can aggravate this heartburn especially in the third trimester when the baby is larger, causing stomach acid to be pushed up to the esophagus. But if that doesn't bother you, try this delicious and spicy smoothie.

Recipe Yields: 3–4 cups

2 cups arugula
1 small jalapeño, seeded
2 small apples of choice, cored and peeled
1 orange, peeled and seeded
½" knob ginger, peeled
2 cups water

1. Combine all ingredients and blend on high until smooth.
2. Add more liquid if necessary.

NUTRITIONAL INFORMATION (PER SERVING SIZE):

CALORIES:	FAT:	PROTEIN:	SODIUM:	CARBOHYDRATES:	SUGAR:	FIBER:
51	0.1 gram	0.7 gram	7 milligrams	13.1 grams	10.2 grams	2.0 grams

Fertility Booster Smoothie

If you are trying to get pregnant, you can start preparing your body for this ultra-important journey. Goodbye to inflammation-causing processed yuck and junk foods. Hello to protein, healthy carbohydrates, good fats, folate, iron, magnesium, and all the other vitamins and nutrients needed to grow a healthy little human.

Recipe Yields: 3–4 cups

2 cups baby spinach
6 figs
½ frozen and peeled banana
¼ cup unsweetened coconut flakes
½" knob ginger, peeled
2 teaspoons raw honey
2 cups coconut water

1. Combine all ingredients and blend on high until smooth.
2. Add more liquid if necessary.

NUTRITIONAL INFORMATION (PER SERVING SIZE):

CALORIES:	FAT:	PROTEIN:	SODIUM:	CARBOHYDRATES:	SUGAR:	FIBER:
129	2.8 grams	1.7 grams	45 milligrams	27.5 grams	22.0 grams	3.4 grams

Stork Alert Smoothie

Many people believe that women who consume a lot of fruits and vegetables (but no bananas) will have a girl because of the magnesium and calcium. Boys are, of course, made from potassium. So, add this to your bag of old wives' tales. The smoothie below has a little of everything, so maybe you'll have twins—a boy and a girl!

Recipe Yields: 3–4 cups

2 cups kale
1 medium banana
1 small carrot, peeled
3 plums, peeled and pitted
1 tablespoon sunflower seeds
2 teaspoons raw honey
2 cups coconut water

1. Combine all ingredients and blend on high until smooth.
2. Add more liquid if necessary.

NUTRITIONAL INFORMATION (PER SERVING SIZE):

CALORIES:	FAT:	PROTEIN:	SODIUM:	CARBOHYDRATES:	SUGAR:	FIBER:
101	1.2 grams	1.8 grams	43 milligrams	22.9 grams	17.1 grams	2.3 grams

Folate for Fine Spines Smoothie

Among the important vitamins and minerals found to prevent birth defects, one of the most well known is folate. Studies have shown that proper levels of folate in pregnancy reduce or remedy the chance of neural and spinal-tube defects. You can take a prenatal vitamin that includes folate, but what about natural sources? Eating a diet rich in deep-green leafy veggies can provide a great amount of folate naturally.

Recipe Yields: 3–4 cups

1½ cups spinach
½ cup chopped broccoli
1 cup diced papaya (make sure the papaya is ripe)
1 cup frozen pineapple chunks
2 cups coconut milk
2 teaspoons raw honey, optional

1. Combine all ingredients and blend on high until smooth.
2. Add more liquid if necessary.

NUTRITIONAL INFORMATION (PER SERVING SIZE):

CALORIES:	FAT:	PROTEIN:	SODIUM:	CARBOHYDRATES:	SUGAR:	FIBER:
267	22.8 grams	3.4 grams	29 milligrams	14.3 grams	4.1 grams	1.8 grams

Pregnant Brain Smoothie

Not only is vitamin C an important addition to your diet for its strong immunity-building power; this vitamin also benefits the expectant mom by providing optimal brain functioning. That means better mental clarity, improved focus, and an overall feeling of awareness instead of the mental fuzziness commonly referred to as "pregnant brain."

Recipe Yields: 3–4 cups

2 cups watercress
2 tangerines or mandarins, peeled and seeded
½ grapefruit, peeled and seeded
½ cup frozen pineapple chunks
½ cup cantaloupe chunks
2 cups red raspberry tea, cooled

1. Combine all ingredients and blend on high until smooth.
2. Add more liquid if necessary.

NUTRITIONAL INFORMATION (PER SERVING SIZE):

CALORIES:	FAT:	PROTEIN:	SODIUM:	CARBOHYDRATES:	SUGAR:	FIBER:
52	0.1 gram	1.2 grams	11 milligrams	13.1 grams	6.1 grams	1.3 grams

Appendix

Standard U.S./Metric Measurement Conversions

VOLUME CONVERSIONS

U.S. Volume Measure	Metric Equivalent
⅛ teaspoon	0.5 milliliter
¼ teaspoon	1 milliliter
½ teaspoon	2 milliliters
1 teaspoon	5 milliliters
½ tablespoon	7 milliliters
1 tablespoon (3 teaspoons)	15 milliliters
2 tablespoons (1 fluid ounce)	30 milliliters
¼ cup (4 tablespoons)	60 milliliters
⅓ cup	80 milliliters
½ cup (4 fluid ounces)	125 milliliters
⅔ cup	160 milliliters
¾ cup (6 fluid ounces)	180 milliliters
1 cup (16 tablespoons)	250 milliliters
1 pint (2 cups)	500 milliliters
1 quart (4 cups)	1 liter (about)

WEIGHT CONVERSIONS

U.S. Weight Measure	Metric Equivalent
½ ounce	15 grams
1 ounce	30 grams
2 ounces	60 grams
3 ounces	85 grams
¼ pound (4 ounces)	115 grams
½ pound (8 ounces)	225 grams
¾ pound (12 ounces)	340 grams
1 pound (16 ounces)	454 grams

OVEN TEMPERATURE CONVERSIONS

Degrees Fahrenheit	Degrees Celsius
200 degrees F	95 degrees C
250 degrees F	120 degrees C
275 degrees F	135 degrees C
300 degrees F	150 degrees C
325 degrees F	160 degrees C
350 degrees F	180 degrees C
375 degrees F	190 degrees C
400 degrees F	205 degrees C
425 degrees F	220 degrees C
450 degrees F	230 degrees C

BAKING PAN SIZES

American	Metric
8 × 1½ inch round baking pan	20 × 4 cm cake tin
9 × 1½ inch round baking pan	23 × 3.5 cm cake tin
11 × 7 × 1½ inch baking pan	28 × 18 × 4 cm baking tin
13 × 9 × 2 inch baking pan	30 × 20 × 5 cm baking tin
2 quart rectangular baking dish	30 × 20 × 3 cm baking tin
15 × 10 × 2 inch baking pan	38 × 25 × 5 cm baking tin (Swiss roll tin)
9 inch pie plate	22 × 4 or 23 × 4 cm pie plate
7 or 8 inch springform pan	18 or 20 cm springform or loose bottom cake tin
9 × 5 × 3 inch loaf pan	23 × 13 × 7 cm or 2 lb narrow loaf or pate tin
1½ quart casserole	1.5 liter casserole
2 quart casserole	2 liter casserole

INDEX

About the Author

Michelle Fagone, a.k.a. "Cavegirl," has a passion for healthy living and for sharing her unique insights via her recipes, her blog, and now her cookbooks. Michelle started CavegirlCuisine.com in March 2012 and has not stopped creating flavorful recipes since. A mother of two, she has an understanding of melding a variety of flavors to please the sometimes picky palates of certain family members.

Michelle is a huge proponent of whole and organic foods, touting their many nutritional and health benefits. While comfort is the basis for most of her recipes, you will often find a twist of exciting flavors, which makes her recipes not only appealing to a broad audience but uniquely delicious—as you will find while flipping through the pages of the Paleo green smoothie combinations in this book.